INVISIBLE IMAGES

INVISIBLE IMAGES

The Silent Language of Architecture
and
the Selected Works of Beverly Willis

with a biography by Nicolai Ouroussoff

DEDICATION
For my brother
R. G. Budd Willis

First published in 1997 by
National Building Museum
Washington, D.C.

ISBN #: 0–9619752–8–8

Printed in Tokyo, Japan by
Dai Nippon Printing Co., Inc.

CONTENTS

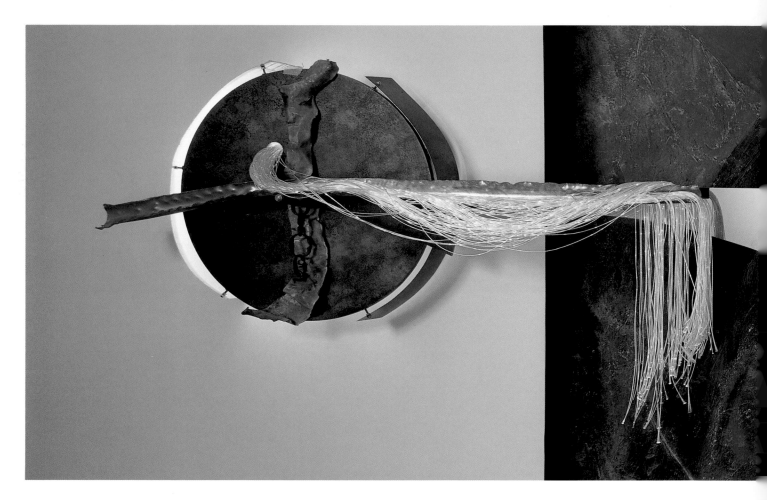

One must be receptive to the image, receptive to the image the moment it appears. — GASTON BACHELARD • *I hope to to*

SURVIVAL, 1991. Construction materials and
fiber optics, 36" x 120". Collection of the artist

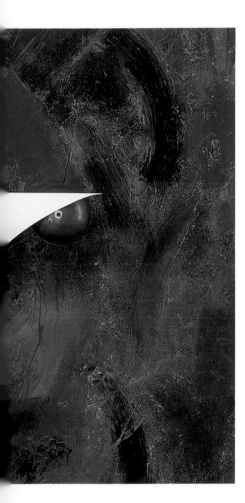

The eighteenth-century German poet and scientist Johann Wolfgang von Goethe once looked at a building and remarked that he saw the rhythms, the harmonies, the swelling crescendos, and the calming rests of a symphony; for him, architecture would always be "frozen music." The great French sculptor Auguste Rodin watched a raven-haired woman drying her locks by a roaring fire and saw twinkling lights in the night sky; to Rodin, the woman's combing gestures imitated "the motion of the stars." The British physicist Sir Isaac Newton observed an apple as it fell from a nearby tree and saw the force of gravity; his insight forever changed how we see the world.

Visual perception of any form—whether the form is created by natural forces or by artistic design—awakens in the imagination an invisible image that imbues sight with meaning. The visible form perceived by the eye and the invisible image conceived by the mind are not one and the same.

Author Norman Mailer tells a joke about two grandmothers who meet while both are pushing baby carriages down the street: "Oh, what a beautiful grandchild you have," says one. "That's nothing," says the other as she reaches for her purse, "Wait 'til I show you her picture."

In the contemporary world, the distinction between the subjective image and the objective form has blurred. From the NBC peacock to the soaring atrium of a Hyatt Hotel, image is form—a prepackaged marketable commodity evoked for collective consumption. Similarly, the phenomenon of the designer-as-celebrity has created an atmosphere in which recognition of a "signature" within a form often matters more than meaningful content. Like the grandchild's photograph, the designer's own image outstrips the viewer's personal engagement with a particular form.

When the invisible images evoked by a form predominantly enhance the recognition of a singular producer (or product or pedagogy), the observer maintains a discreet distance from the work. Just as memorization is not comprehension, recognition is not revelation. Understanding *why* this transformation exists requires far more intellectual, emotional, and creative investment than simply recognizing who created it and what it represents. In a world where instant recognition is the general expectation, an eight-second "sight bite" reveals no more than an eight-second sound bite.

Architects, sculptors, choreographers, graphic designers, and cinematographers

ething of people in my designs, to connect with how people feel and sense that which surrounds them. — BEVERLY WILLIS •

SURVIVAL

In the discarded debris of renovation, I saw a sculpture. Salvaged materials, such as lead pipe that housed turn-of-the-century copper telephone wire and delicate strands of contemporary fiber optics, juxtapose old and new in a visual narrative of the building's historical evolution.

share a desire to reveal the not-yet-seen: the invisible forces that affect human experience. For art to have any meaningful place in contemporary society, visible forms and their invisible images must engage the viewer in a subjective dialogue with the work—a dialogue sensed and felt through the depth and dimension of invisible images rather than merely recognized in surface appearance.

My work explores the invisible images that are both precursors and progeny of observed forms. As an architect, artist, sculptor, writer, and urbanist, I seek the communicative power of these images and their related forms. To discover the power of a specific shape, I may explore the image's essence in two-dimensional abstract geometries, in poetic sketches, in three-dimensional architectonics, or in a combination of media. The images' essential characteristics carry over from one project—or medium—to the next. I attempt to create works that transcend the boundaries of aesthetic theory or formal manipulation and that invite multiple interpretations.

For years, I accentuated the corner details on door and window openings, thinking this an original and clever idea. After exploring the experiential threads

of these images, however, I came to believe that my tendency to elaborate corners came from my early architectural studies. I believed that Michelangelo's sketch for the detailed Casa Buonarroti portal was the precursor of my corners.

Some years later—at the request of a biographer—I began searching through old photographs to rediscover the places of my childhood. Behind my parents, loomed my family's brick house—complete with crisp square details at the window corners. Which invisible image from which point in my life was I communicating in my work? Even I can't say for sure.

This book follows the same course, posing questions rather than offering definitive answers. The essay is an example of associative thinking. The various sections assemble and associate unexpected subjects in to suggest connections. (*Architectural project information is located on pages 106-9.*) The text explores how visible form communicates through invisible images, uniting artist, observer, form, and event. Rather than relying solely on masterpieces from art (and architectural) history, the visual "text" draws largely from my own work: my own invisible images, which span a wide range of media. Together, the

visual and verbal texts provide a free-flowing harmony of thematic parts, a conversation between images and words.

I invite the reader to enter the dialogue and interpret the possibilities: to see beyond the image on the page and discover an imagined other.

Beverly Willis
New York, New York

BELOW LEFT TO RIGHT:
Detail from the Goeglein Pool House; Michelangelo's study for Casa Buonarroti portal, Florence, Italy; and Willis family portrait.

I own the world because I understand it. — BALZAC • *Art does not render what is visible, but renders visible.* — EDGAR D

Vision: the art of seeing things invisible. — JONATHAN SWIFT

THE SILENT LANGUAGE OF ARCHITECTURE

From the sidewalks of Boston's Back Bay to those of San Francisco's Nob Hill, evening strollers wander by townhouses that were built in bygone eras. Light from mullioned windows spills out onto the pavement, inviting passersby to look beyond the glass. One person "sees" an image of earlier days: an intimate gathering before a roaring fire or rainy days spent reading hard-bound books in an overstuffed chair. Another person "sees" tension: ailing grandparents who want freedom from infirmity or multicultural residents whose lifestyles and backgrounds don't mesh with the traditional American neighborhood. Yet another sees physical reality: single-pane windows leaking heat, brickwork in need of tuckpointing, endless investment in maintenance and upkeep.

Poet Nicholas Carpenter wrote in his poem "Midsummer":

Floating by the park at dusk, through
the heavy trees,
the white building glides like a ship.

An amber lamp is lit in a top floor
window
and a woman in her robe is leaning on
the sill, eyes closed to the sunset.

A violet shadow is pouring down the
side of the building from her long
hair.

Two pigeons are perched in the next
window, against a black room.

Are these "seen" images stored in memories, associated with past experience, or imagined events? However vague and fleeting, however clear or precise, physical perception combines with creative imagination to generate individually conceived images. These invisible semblances constitute a silent nonverbal language—a split-second visual communication—that connects observer and observed, reinforcing or challenging the observer's subjective experiences and unconscious preferences through instantaneous and often intense reaction.

What do those strollers *really* see from their sidewalk vantage point? Depending on the particular block of a particular city, they see an assemblage of Second Empire, Federal, Georgian, neoclassical, Victorian, or modern structures in varying states of stylistic authenticity. Some of the edifices emphasize mass and weight, such as brownstones with their rich surfaces and deep shadows. Others stress balance and symmetry, their brick facades delicately accentuated by subtle alterations in bond patterns. Some have mansard roofs, their gray and green slate tiles fish-scaling down the steep slopes; some are made of wood and appear to have no roofs at all, their flat tops concealed behind exaggerated projecting cornices or parapet walls. Such descriptions constitute the spoken language used by the historian, preservationist, or construction detailer—"realistic" descriptions that may accurately convey a neighborhood's surface appearance. Yet these images offer no sense of the area's feel: whether it is comfortable or threatening, harmonious or discordant, approachable or diffident.

While the light from the townhouse window attracts passersby, not all strollers will accept the invitation to look within. To see the townhouse is to perceive its visible appearance, to read its nonverbal language—as most strollers do. To see into the house is to conceive an invisible presence beyond the surface, to discover a deeper real-

at images have both a history and a prehistory; they are always a blend of memory and legend, with the result that we never

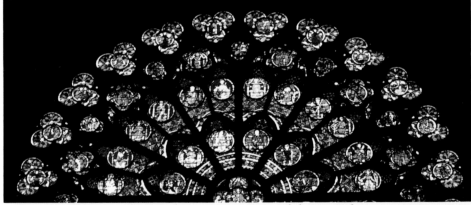

experience an image directly. — GASTON BACHELARD • *The art of a people is a true mirror of their minds.* — JAWAHARLAL NEH

ity or silent language within the form.

Little is known about the connections between observation, imagination, invention, and interpretation. History records events such as Sir Isaac Newton's discovery of gravity, inspired by his observation of a falling apple. In that moment, an invisible connection occurred, resulting in a discovery that changed the course of science.

Marcus Vitruvius Pollio, the first-century Roman engineer-architect and author of *De Architectura*, told the story of a nurse in Corinth who after the burial of her mistress put a basket of her favorite things on her tomb and covered it with a roof tile, which forced an acanthus root beneath it to produce leaves and stalks that curled downward as they grew. Seeing this and using the stunted plant as a model, the craftsman chiseled a timeless image in stone: this chance observation inspired the concept of the Corinthian column capital.

Similarly, an anonymous eleventh-century stained-glass craftsman stopped to look at a daisy while strolling down a country lane. He noticed the how the petals radiated from the circular stamen. Perhaps, in that brief moment, he "saw" the design for the Rose Window of the Gothic cathedral of Notre Dame de Paris. (*See the* Rose Window, *on the opposite page, below; and the* Daisy Morph *on page 2.*)

All art forms seek to reveal or express the invisible, unarticulated, and often unperceived forces that affect the human experience at a given time: from architecture to music, dance to painting, drama to sculpture, cinematography to illustration. Objects that command attention and communicate at some profound level become timeless, weaving a tapestry of universal expression. The invisible images surrounding such forms or designs not only distinguish the present from the past but generate new possibilities between heuristics (discovery) and hermeneutics (interpretation).

A panoply of images exists within the designer's mind. Some are memories of personal experiences, some derive from current events, and some are archetypal images from collective experience; others link generations through oral history. The relation between experience, knowledge, memories, and images is a kind of invisible image — a web of connections yet to be made — a type of visual architecture in itself.

The designer (or form maker) identifies essential traits within these invisible images and transforms them through various means—line, color, shape, rhythm, texture, extension, juxtaposition, and opposition—into visible form. These elements interact with each other, one altering the next in a silent dialogue of abstracted visual language.

The fundamental elements of Theo van Doesburg's De Stijl—an early Dutch modernist movement—were the straight line, the right angle, the cross and the point, rectangular planes and convertible plastic space, the three primary colors—red, blue, and yellow—a white ground with black and gray, and black lines. Using

FACING PAGE:
(above) Detail of a daisy. (below) Detail of the Rose Window at the Cathedral of Notre Dame de Paris.

THIS PAGE:
TRIPTYCH VOCABULARY. Oil on masonite. 9" x 41". Collection of the artist.

nce and art belong to the whole world, and before them vanish the barriers of nationality. — JOHANN WOLFGANG VON GOETHE

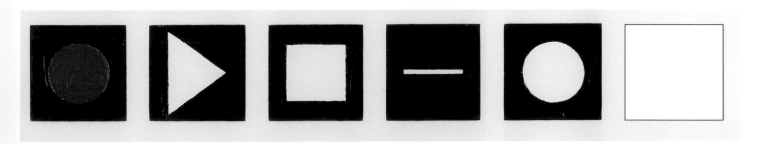

these rudimentary tools, De Stijl artists intended to represent and construct essential harmony, the nature of which was understood somewhat differently by various group members. For artist Piet Mondrian, harmony was a quasi-mystical universal absolute. For architect Gerrit Rietveld, harmony was formal balance and the implied social meaning that he hoped to achieve in a particular work.

Influenced by the studies of Wassily Kandinsky and Paul Klee, I created a "visual language" alphabet to compose images out of the vast number of abstract words: concepts currently disassociated from visual imagery. Verbs like *am, be, was, want, become, create*; adjectives like *invisible, intimate, beautiful, comfortable, threatening*; and nouns like *love, imagination, character, virtue, truth*, and *justice* are usually given meaning by usage, context, or accepted definition.

I defined each image. The point/line means a moving point that possesses a beginning and end: a connector between two points. The circle/mass means oneness: a wholeness such as the universe or universes-within-universes: the identity as a whole. The point/circle defines the process of becoming. The square/rectangle

defines enclosure or a limited transformation field. The triangle refers to a force that can "affect," causing change. The blank field or space represents infinite space, either an inner or outer space—or transformation field. Color represents an identity and its tone. Black and white are opposite extremes from which all other hues gradate and recede. I used the same primary color palette as the De Stijl artists, but I applied both white and black backgrounds and did not specify line weight or color.

I painted triptychs with these alphabetic definitions. Introducing the image in a three-frame sequence—like the segmented motion of a filmstrip—allows a viewer to interpret a meaning. (*See* Transformation Triptychs *on pages 18, 20, 38, 45, 50, 75, 79, and 88.*)

While the graphic images for plastic space (that is, space not created by perspective), a circle/dot, a line (a dot in motion), a square/rectangle, a triangle, and colors differed only slightly from that of the De Stijl artists, my interpretation was radically different.

Years later, when scientist Benoit Mandelbrot's fractal studies were published, I observed certain similarities between my

alphabet and the "natural" composition of fractals.

Although each art form and subject matter has its own disciplinary tradition, each artist interprets essential characteristics in his or her own way. That interpretation becomes rooted in his or her subconscious. I observed this in my own work when I realized the extent to which my abstract two-dimensional painting influenced my three-dimensional architectural form.

Rene Magritte's painting *Clairvoyance* is another example of transformation from invisible image to visible form. The painting depicts an artist looking at an egg and painting a bird. The artist's inner eye "sees" the potential bird within the egg. By connecting the actual with the potential, the artist gives the implied bird physical reality—visually employing a metaphor to represent the invisible process of transformation. (*See Magritte's* Clairvoyance, *below.*)

We establish a threshold of awakenings. We choose how stark a truth we are willing to adjust into consciousness, how readi

RENE MAGRITTE, *Clairvoyance*, 1936. Oil on Canvas, 54 x 65 cm, Private Collection, courtesy Galerie Isy Brachot, Brussels.

Man's search to reveal the essential forces inherent in the natural world includes the representation of human forces. The *Venus of Willendorf*, a stone effigy dating from 26,000–20,000 B.C., is an archetypal depiction of the power of woman. This figurine evokes the female form via a cluster of highly abstracted elliptical shapes. This earth goddess is heavy with a tangible fecundity, ripe with the fertile possibility of new life. Henry Moore's *Reclining Figure: Festival* (1951) recalls a gentle landscape of rolling hills and curvaceous valleys. Unmistakably female, the forms suggest both earth and woman. The great earth mother—source of all life—transcends the span of centuries since the upper Paleolithic era to reappear in undulating wood. The invisible image is old; the visible transformation is new.

Visible form has traditionally celebrated the double-sided archetype of female and male. Whether representing physical attributes or questioning cultural attitudes, forms reveal the essential forces of sensual power and sexual dynamism of human experience. When juxtaposed within one form, the interplay of invisible forces (which is culturally labeled as either feminine or masculine) takes on a palpable tension that

unites the two modes of being into an integrated whole. We experience the suppleness of feminine possibility simultaneously with the rigidity of masculine strength. The feminine curve plays against the masculine angle, the void plays against the mass in a yin/yang of promise and power, creativity and control.

In my design for the San Francisco Ballet Building, the rigid rectilinearity of the columnar facade is juxtaposed against the swelling curves of the balconies and the rippling reflections of the glass walls, creating a natural tension between complements. Solid and void, curve and plane play in constantly shifting light and shadows. The monumentality of the mass is softened by transparent layers that reveal an inner space of creative possibility, awaiting the birth of the dance. The two aspects intertwine, each a part of the other in an endless choreography of female and male, point and counterpoint, movement and rest. (*See the* San Francisco Ballet Building *on pages 16–25.*)

In the Western world, the sociopolitical evolution of cultural traditions has separated and compartmentalized these homogenous aspects of human nature into discrete—and often stereotyped—oppositions. In dance,

the feminine and masculine natures synthesize, or merge, through form and motion.

This classical image of ballet and the neoclassical context of the San Francisco Ballet Building's Civic Center location merge in the structure's design through form and detail. Yet in the tall entry columns that support balcony canopies, I can "see" the trunks of stalwart redwood trees, invisibly connecting the natural world and human forces.

(below, left) VENUS OF WILLENDORF. Collection of the Museum of Natural History, Vienna Austria. Courtesy of the Artists Rights Society.
(below, right) HENRY MOORE, *Reclining Figure: Festival*, 1951. Reproduced by permission of the Henry Moore Foundation.

examine the contradictions of our lives and beliefs. — MARILYN FERGUSON • *The threshold ... sustains the middle in which the*

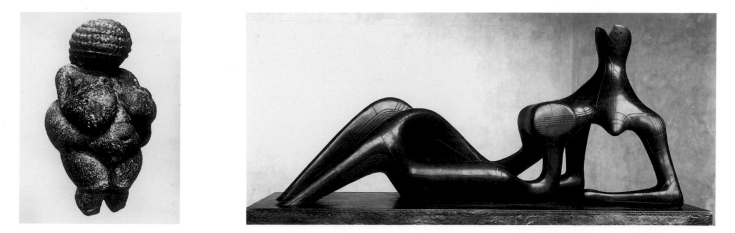

two, the outside and the inside, penetrate each other. — MARTIN HEIDEGGER • *As the choreographer uses movement, the hur*

SAN FRANCISCO BALLET
ASSOCIATION BUILDING

Like towering redwoods with their leafy canopies, monumental columns with curving balconies form the facade of the San Francisco Ballet Association Building. Light filters past these columns, offering a glimpse into the lobby within. The building awaits the animating moment—the arrival of the dancer, the soaring leap of the dancer's rehearsal.

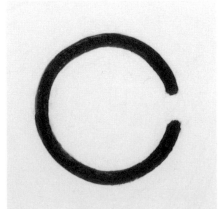

body, and space to create images of magic, beauty, and harmony, I used both the Renaissance and the inspirational elements

Transformation Triptych
Parthenogenesis

The point/line moving is the process
of becoming, whether a force (represented
by a triangle), an enclosure (symbolized by a
square), or an identity (depicted by a circle),
like the development of an egg without
fertilization.

ce to create the ballet building. — BEVERLY WILLIS • *If a man does not keep pace with his companions, perhaps it is because he*

BALLET

… I saw ballet as a composition of female and male forms—soft and hard—of curved lines and edges that are supple, sensuous, and seductive. I saw flowing arcs of gesture frozen in stone, steel, and glass. A building whose white, glistening stone surface was stretched taut, as the body when lifting weight, as when two males held the female dancer high above their heads. I thought of tall columns articulating the facade, defining the entry…and curved balconies softly breaking the hard edge of the stone. I imagined the play of sunlight, like theatrical lights, making ever-changing shadows that would animate the surfaces, the deep-set voids of the windows and the curving, transparent glass entry. Within I saw the two-story spaces filled with choreographed movement, awaiting new possibilities.

hears a different drummer. Let him step to the music which he hears, however measured or far away. — HENRY DAVID THOREA

THIS PAGE:
(above) Detail of ceiling.

FACING PAGE:
(above) Detail of curved window.
(below) Bird morph.

etter to create than to be learned, creating is the true essence of life. — BARTHOLD GEORG NIEBUHR • *Increasing sensitiveness to*

these mysteries by means of intuition, instinct, and imagination, is the essential thing in the search for form. — ELIEL SAARINEN

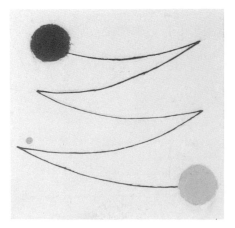

Transformation Triptych
Extension

The point/line moves or extends at an angled bounce off an identity (depicted by a rectangle), creating spatial tension as it sways back and forth, floating downward.

THIS PAGE:
(left) TRANSFORMATION TRIPTYCH. Oil on masonite. 6" × 6". Collection of the artist.
(right) Lobby interior.

FACING PAGE:
Exterior view of lobby.

re looking for something to be brave about, consider the fine arts. — ROBERT FROST • *All thinking creates images.* — ARISTOTLE

MOTION

... I saw the frothing edge of a crested wave as it receded on the sand, drawing an undulating line of glistening bubbles. As the waves pounded unceasingly, they created a rhythmic cycle, leaving imprints on the sand: tracing patterns of motion, as if they were drawn on the textured sand like that of rough stucco walls.

• *Man is the measure of all things, of being things that they exist, and of nonentities that they do not exist.* — PROTAGORAS •

THIS PAGE:
(above) Exterior stucco wall of rear drive-through entry.

FACING PAGE:
Exterior. Sculpture by Walter Dusenbery.

...o created man after his own image; for as the world is the image of God, so man is the image of the world. — H. CORNELIUS

SACRED AND PROFANE

Comparative themes are as old as both oral and recorded history, uniting all cultures in the search to give meaning, purpose, and potential to daily life. Sacred and profane, natural and geometric, organic and intentional, feminine and masculine, myth and narration, illusion and reality, order and chaos all represent timeless constructs of interrelated forces. The relationships between these paired elements invert, subvert, and revert in response to the sociocultural norms of each place and time. When the artist's subjective interpretation and transformation make this dynamic visible, viewers can connect personal experience with visible form to generate countless interpretations.

Faced with apparently random events and a mysterious unknown, humanity has always sought a higher meaning or purpose for existence. Early civilizations intuitively grasped distinctive or recurring events and imagined another, "higher" order. Although manifested in objects that were part of the natural—or profane—world, this wholly different order is now commonly know as the sacred. By manifesting this higher order, an object becomes something else while remaining itself. A sacred stone was revered because it represented another state of being, simultaneously expressing two modalities of human experience.

The archetype of the sacred and the profane is primordial. The invisible presence of this other world has held such power that even the earliest functional objects were transformed by invisible images into a sacred order. The main lodge pole of an American Indian dwelling was not merely a functional support but an *axis mundi* that connected the world below, the world within, and the world above. The hole in the roof did not merely allowed rising smoke to escape but facilitated spiritual passage from one world to the next. The entry tunnel to this shelter allow the "spirit" of the outer world to be filtered and transformed into an inner, unifying self within: all those who sought warmth and security were transformed.

Similarly, my earliest art represented and revealed a higher invisible order. Abstraction and imagination gave the intangible construct of the sacred tangible form. Spiritual passage between worlds is embodied in my fresco, entitled *Descending Dove,* which I painted for the United Church of Christ in Honolulu. Since the birth of Christianity, the dove has symbolized the Holy Ghost—an invisible participant in the ceremonial communion that is celebrated by believers. The dove glides downward, bathed in shafts of light, symbolizing the promise of everlasting life. (*See* Descending Dove *on page 27.*)

Ancient Hawaiian cultures used *ki'i*—human figures carved of wood, often of towering height—as symbolic receptacles of certain spirits. Interpreting this imagery, I carved a 300-pound koa wood *ki'i* for the United Air Lines ticket office in Waikiki. I intended this figure to serve as a symbolic protective talisman for travelers who passed through the office. (*See* Ki'i *on page 27.*)

From totems to sphinxes, canoes to cross-beams, other early art forms acknowledged the sacred in the profane. Sculpted deities—half natural, half "otherworld"—gained cultural reverence. Artists lavished their talents on the masks and ritual garbs for ceremonial dances. When worn, these powerful creations did not simply disguise the dancer as a likeness of an animal spirit but enabled that dancer to become the animal.

Inspired by mythological Chinese dragons, I made a mixed-media work, entitled *Dragon Dancer*: the effigy of the magical

AGRIPPA • *Through every rift of discovery some seeming anomaly drops out of the darkness, and falls, as a golden link, into the*

FACING PAGE:
(left to right) DESCENDING DOVE, 1956. Fresco, 30" x 60". United Church of Christ, Honolulu, Hawaii; *Ki'i,* 1958. Carved koa wood, approx. 36" x 48". United Airlines, Waikiki, Honolulu, Hawaii; and STONE DRAGON GOD, 1965. Ceramic and lava stones, 18" x 48". Private collection of Douglas McMahon.

of order. — EDWIN HUBBEL CHAPIN • *Ideas are the root of creation.* — ERNEST DIMNET • *The artist does not ascribe to the natur-*

DESCENDING DOVE

Since the birth of Christianity, the dove has symbolized the Holy Ghost, an invisible participant in ceremonial communion with believers. Seen bathed in shafts of light, a dove glides downward, symbolizing the promise of everlasting life.

THE KI'I

Ancient Hawaiian cultures used *Ki'i*, human figures carved of wood and often of towering height, as symbolic receptacles of certain spirits. The artist's personal memory fuses with this traditional imagery to create a striking sculpture.

STONE DRAGON GOD

A magical beast formed of cast ceramic pieces and lava stones, with eyes of molten glass that flash in the sunlight, draws its inspiration from the mythological Chinese dragon.

beast that symbolizes fortune and the "Son of Heaven." (*See the* Dragon God *on page 27.*)

In early art, mystical creatures with animal heads and human bodies (or vice versa) created the illusion of a shared existence between these two life forms. Anthropomorphic figures of the gods implied a personal connection between the deities and human beings, and hence between heaven and earth. In each case, the terror of the unknown "other world" was balanced by a recognizable identity from this world, expressing a double-sided archetype.

Psychologist Carl Jung believed that all myths convey the archetypal struggle between good and evil in the psyche: the mythical fire-breathing dragon is the shadowy side found deep within each personality. The animal within is filled with destructive tendencies that must be overcome by the human that desires to grasp the values of the higher mind. Mythical narratives present both sides of this archetype, each shadowing the other. The central figure or figures—with all of the vulnerabilities of natural, mortal life—must recognize the power of the opposing force. Vulnerability—by drawing strength

from its opposite—gains protection. The anthropomorphic figure becomes supernatural.

In our modern, secular world, trace images can be found within some archetypal forms that depict the simultaneity of sacred and profane. The sacred roof opening that leads the way to spiritual passage appears in both the Pantheon's oculus and the cupolas of Italianate mansions. The *axis mundi* reappears as the pristine spire of a New England church and as the stark pillar of the Washington Monument. In Alberti's church at Sant' Andrea, two motifs—the triumphal arch and the temple front—lock in a dynamic play of sacred and secular.

In an effort to create a tangible example of this concept, I transformed a profane object—a functional chair—into a sacred, ritualistic place by incorporating geometric proportions and expanding its scale. Exhibited at the Cooper Hewitt Museum, New York, Athena's Chaise simultaneously accommodates the finite world of humanity and the infinite world of the gods. It serves as both object and context. It is utilitarian and ceremonial. It defies singular categorization by hovering in between the two worlds each per-

son finds within his or her own soul. (*See* Athena's Chaise *on pages 29–30.*)

---

al form of appearance the same significance as the realists who are his critics. — PAUL KLEE • *The images of myth are reflections*

ual potential in every one of us. —JOSEPH CAMPBELL • *The most beautiful emotion we can experience is the mystical.* — ALBERT

EINSTEIN • *We have abolished superstitions of the heart only to install a superstition of the intellect in its place.* — LAURENS VA

ATHENA'S CHAISE

Expanded in scale, a utilitarian lawn chair
becomes a gazebo for the gods, a private
Olympus for the heroic few. Ritual space
and functional object combine to create a
chair fit for Athena, transporting the sitter
to an imaginary realm.

Traditionally, a myth tells the story of how something came into being. The mysteries surrounding the origins of the world, of men and women, of life and death, of natural disasters and unnatural paradise are all explained in a revelation of supernatural forces and events.

Myths represent the supernatural world. Narrative represents the natural world: the world of ordinary humans and daily life. Part of the oral traditions drawn from human experience and imagination, the double-sided archetype of myth and narrative becomes, in turn, the basis of artistic storytelling through form and decoration.

The Mr. and Mrs. Richard Goeglein Pool House in California's Napa Valley is an example, located on a site rumored to be a former campsite of the Wappa tribe. Researchers found nothing visually iconic in the Wappa traditions. These indigenous people were wanderers, gatherers, and hunters. They apparently either cast their work in such impermanent materials as weavings and wood or never stopped long enough to build or mark their habitats. In the design of the building, I created a mythical narrative. Lacking Wappa symbols, I reinterpreted ancient Egyptian mythology using Napa Valley imagery.

Under the stucco skin of the building exterior walls, I inserted symbolic notations, creating an illusion of windows and columns in the style of ancient funerary decoration. On the south elevation, facing a sculptural monument to the Wappa tribe, I designed a narrative wall, which tells how the spirit-soul of the dead floated in a sky boat from earth to the heavens. (*See* Goeglein Pool House wall *on pages 32, 36–37, and 41–42.*)

Visible form appears in full simultaneity to the observer. The human eye perceives the object and its context as inextricably linked. Without that context, the object has little meaning. Architecture as an art form cannot escape the attribution of the multiple meanings: of the deep structure of human consciousness and unconscious thought. Reduction to architectural forms, surfaces, and details ignore the natural, instinctive interpretations of deep meaning is meaningless.

The pool house building was constructed near a stone mound rumored to be an Indian grave. To commemorate the passing of the Wappa tribe, Richard Goeglein wished to create a monument. An oblique wall was constructed around the stone mound with one half of the wall

built several feet higher than the other. In the sculpture—which symbolizes a native dwelling lodge pole—a circular disk centered on the mound connects the world below, the world within, and the world above. By orienting the sculpture to the summer solstice's noonday sun, the shadow of the spirit disk—symbolic of the soul—dwells on the grave during the day. As the sun moves west, the spirit shadow moves across the stones, across the green and purple painted horizon on the semicircular wall to the painted blue sky.

The shadow trace of a Wappa tribesman spirit materializes from the ether at sunrise, flourishes in the dappled light of day, and passes from sight at dusk, awaiting rebirth the next day: a daily ritual that ends with the last solstice sun. Is it a day in the span of life or life in the span of a day? A story of mortality or of immortality? (*See* Goeglein Sculpture *on pages 35–40.*)

Critical of the anthropomorphic gods and goddesses of Homeric myth—and perhaps more than a bit envious of their popular appeal—the ancient Greek philosopher and mythographer Euhermerus posited that myths simply represent an imaginative transfiguration that deified ancient kings and

• *Architecture is how the design appears to the eye and feels to the mind and the touch of the body.* — BEVERLY WILLIS • *We*

shape our buildings, therefore they shape us. — WINSTON CHURCHILL • *No architecture can be truly noble which is not imperfe*

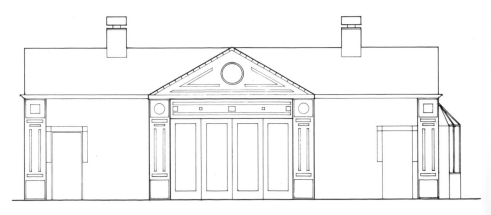

GOEGLEIN POOL HOUSE

Deeply carved in earthy stucco on the sun-drenched russet red facade of a bath house, mythological runes pay tribute to the site's lost history. Geometric lines, circles, and planes, like those on a funerary box, create an illusion of windows and columns. Sculpted on the south wall, a mural tells a story of a spirit-carrying skyboat setting sail from its Napa Valley shores, returning the soul of the dead to the heavens as the sun sets. Sliding doors slip into wall pockets, dissolving the boundaries between the pool and the house. Within stands a fireplace emitting the crackle of dry wood and the fragrance of burning eucalyptus.

HN RUSKIN • *In using myth one must take care not to confuse image with fact, which would be like climbing up the signpost*

FACING PAGE:
(top left) Building isonometric; (top right) Goeglein Pool House exterior; and (bottom) rear elevation.

THIS PAGE:
Pool house interior.

instead of following the road. — ALAN WATTS • *The magical working symbol is required, containing that primitive analogy*

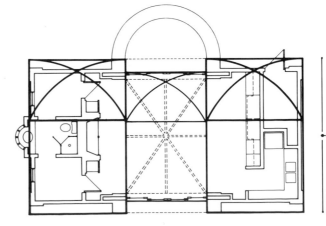

s to the unconscious in its very own language ... and whose goal is to unite the singularity of contemporary consciousness

THIS PAGE:
Goeglein sculpture.

FACING PAGE:
(top to bottom) Goeglein Pool house interior
view looking toward the pool; Golden section
analysis of elevation.

NEXT SPREAD:
Pool House and sculpture.

GOEGLEIN SCULPTURE

A circular disk symbolic of a spirit-soul is placed above a rock-covered mound circled by a low, ringlike wall, part of which rises higher than the mound. Shadows of a nearby oak tree cast cloudlike reflections against the high, painted blue wall. Rising to meet the dappled summer solstice sun, the marker's shadow begins its spiritual journey, dwelling during the day on the rocky mound, moving as the sun sets in the west across the painted horizon to the wall sky and beyond to the heavens.

with life's most ancient past. — CARL JUNG • *Supreme art is a traditional statement of certain heroic and religious truths, pe*

ge to age, modified by individual genius, but never abandoned. — WILLIAM BUTLER YEATS • *The history of European Archi-*

SHADOWS

…I thought of the main lodge pole of an American Indian dwelling, which was considered an *axis mundi* that connected the world below, the world within, and the world above. Since earliest times builders have erected a pole on the building site and studied the length and depth of its shadow to orientate the building to the sun and to connect it with heavenly forces. I thought how shadows painted bas-relief sculptural incisions. I wanted the sculpture to capture the summer solstice sun shadow as it moved, rising, dwelling on the rocky earth, and setting in a red-orange glow at the end of a long day, ending in the dark silence of night.

tecture is the history of the struggles with the window. — LE CORBUSIER • *In mythology, life on earth is a beginning, death*

THIS PAGE:
TRANSFORMATION TRIPTYCH. Oil on masonite. 6"x6". Collection of the artist.

FACING PAGE:
Sculpture detail.

Transformation Triptych
Character

An identity (circle) sits in a transformation field (rectangle) within a second transformation field (square). Its tone is defined by its color. Its character changes as it moves from light to dark. The degree of character change is proportionate to the extent of the movement through the transformation fields.

station, a bridge to an eternal and wonderful existence. — BEVERLY WILLIS • *New principles do not fall from heaven, but*

are logically if indirectly connected with past and future. What is important to us is the momentary position of the principle and

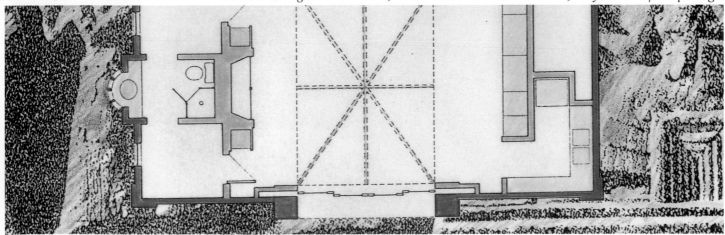

can be used. — WASSILY KANDINSKY • *The sun turning into the moon, which in turn becomes the sun, is symbolic of the passage*

of the soul through space and time. — BEVERLY WILLIS • *Perhaps in the end we shall discover that though the interpretations ar*

queens and monumentalized their exploits. As early philosophers strove to separate objective reality from subjective experience, the Greek word *mythos* acquired the same derisive connotations as our modern disdain for the term *illusion*. In the "real" world of the Greeks, myth meant "what cannot really exist." Despite such attacks, the power of the myths persisted. The stories were modified and the names changed, but the appeal of the myths was unshakable, for they revealed the sacred, ideal, and illusory other of human experience.

Reenacting and retelling a myth in a new form makes a connection, expressing a continuity of life. We know that visible form that reveals a personal connection with the forces common to all human experience engages, captivates, and awes the observer. We revere these forms because they heighten both individual identity and empathy with the collective whole, expanding personal understanding of the world at a moment in time.

For example, the design of the Goeglein Pool House used the golden section (*see page 34*). The proportion (the radical of 5.1 divided by 2)—which was called the "Section" by the ancient Greeks, the "Divine Proportion" by Luca Pacioli

(1509), and the "Golden Section" by artist-architect Leonardo da Vinci and his followers—has unique properties. The golden section exists between two measurable quantities of any kind when the ratio between the larger and the smaller is equal to the ratio between the sum of the two and the larger one. In geometric terms, it may be easily generated from the double square.

Double-sided archetypes, like the patterns demonstrated by chaos theory, remain constant over time – continuous universal forces. Only the particular form changes. Spanning the range of human experience, form becomes a powerful vehicle for identity and inclusion, a masterpiece bridging the cracks and fractured ideologies that threaten to shatter our fragile cultural mosaic.

ent, they are complimentary and not contradictory. —UMBERTO ECO • *Order is not repetition. It is a central idea.* — LOUIS KAHN

ILLUSION AND REALITY

All art is illusion: it can never be the thing it represents. A painting that depicts the forces of democracy, for instance, cannot be those actual forces. The portrait of a person is not that actual person. As René Magritte boldly stated on a painting of a pipe, "Ceci n'est pas une pipe." Yet works of art intending to portray an objective physical actuality differ from works meant to convey a hyperreality beyond actual material appearance.

A museum board reviewed a painting by James McNeill Whistler for inclusion in its permanent collection. One board member remained bitterly opposed to accepting the work, complaining that he had never seen a sunset look that way. "Yes," Whistler replied, "but don't you wish you had?"

Illusion is the wonder world of the invisible, offering insight into the glories of a sunset or the terrors of the gods. Illusion in art heightens the personal experience of visible form through a silent language. Is it a dream or a reality? A sleight of the artist's hand or a very real quirk of nature?

Trained as a goldsmith (with occasional forays into painting and sculpture), Renaissance architect Filippo Brunelleschi is popularly credited with inventing perspective.

By combining mathematical with pictorial principles, Brunelleschi generated a system of two-dimensional representation that gives the illusion of spatial depth, dissolving the picture's finite plane into an infinite space.

Centuries later, photography reinforced the notion that perspective is reality, not merely an illusion of artistic convention. The clarity of the photograph and the cultural conventions that led to its invention presume to mirror actual sight.

My interior design for the Greenwich Apartment—a renovation situated on San Francisco's Telegraph Hill—resonates with the alternating presence of reality and illusion. With minor demolition and reconstruction, I transformed the dark, cramped spaces of the existing layout through painted perspective, mirrored reflections, trompe l'oeil, *faux* painting, and artificial lighting, creating an overall illusion of an expansive, sun-washed space. *(See* Greenwich Apartment *on pages 45 to 50.)*

Thickening wall openings and introducing heavy columns and pilasters sacrificed precious floor space. Yet the substantial weight and heightened detail evoke spaces of a far grander scale. The interior's elegance and visual richness belie the actual cost of the design in a sophisticated play between sensory illusion and material reality.

The white, purple, and ochre hues of the stippled walls—tints harmonious with the quality of light—change the "seen" wall color as the outdoor light changes. In brilliant sunlight, the walls appear to be white; in cloudy weather, they turn blue-gray; and at sunrise, they turn golden. The waters of San Francisco Bay reflect in the windows of buildings on the opposite shore, shimmering against the walls and mirroring the motion of the waves.

One wanders through this changing interior landscape, seeing into its gleaming countertops, polished mirrors, and painted illusions: some visions are fleeting, others are permanent. But there is always something different.

To the reality-obsessed Greeks, such an illusion would have been synonymous with delusion: an artificial and deceptive product of the imagination that would crumble under the weight of objective evidence.

There's none so blind as they that won't see. — JONATHAN SWIFT • *What is history but a fable agreed upon?* — NAPOLEON BONAPAR[TE]

Transformation Triptych
Transition

An identity (circle) floats in space (enclosure), which is changed by the appearance of a second enclosure. Disrupted by an exterior force (triangle), the identity shifts its position, tilting—making a transition.

e association of two or more apparently alien elements on a plane alien to both is the potent ignition of poetry. — MAX ERNST •

Faith is, above all, openness—an act of trust in the unknown. — ALAN WATTS • *Because the mind's eye scales by contrasting some*

GREENWICH APARTMENT

Reflected in the water of the bay and in the windows on the opposite shore, the oranges, pinks, and purples of the sunset fill a panoramic window with jeweled light. Inside, gleaming countertops, polished mirrors, and stippled walls change color in a shimmering dance with dusk. As one wanders through this landscape, illusions—some fleeting, some permanent—both delight and surprise the inner eye.

THIS PAGE:
View of San Francisco Bay from the dining area.

FACING PAGE:
Stairwell detail..

wn with something familiar, the mind superimposes the known image on the unknown and concludes that the image is of a cer-

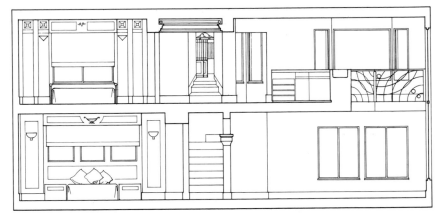

tain size. — BEVERLY WILLIS • *The man who cannot visualize a horse galloping on a tomato is an idiot.* — ANDRÉ BRETON • *Bu*

THIS PAGE:
(above) Bedroom. (middle) Second floor section. (below) First floor section.

FACING PAGE:
Hallway mural.

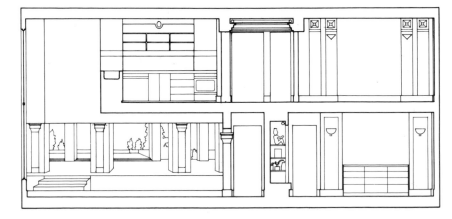

ILLUSIONS

... Images reflected in the waters of San Francisco Bay bounce through the two-story window of the apartment. I saw them merging with the trompe l'oeil, *faux*, and stippled walls—illusions sliding over mirrored surfaces where the real and reflected merge. Perspectives become other perspectives. Space melts forms, invisibly shaping other images.

st thing of all is to be master of the metaphor...because a good metaphor implies the intuitive perception of similarity in dissimi-

Transformation Triptych
Connection

Three different identities (circles) occupy
the same space. Two of them choose to
connect (line, connector). The third one
then joins the other two.

lar things. — ARISTOTLE • *Art is a form of catharsis.* — DOROTHY PARKER • *The more minimal the art, the more maximum the ex*

 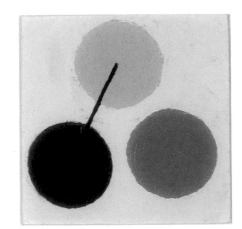 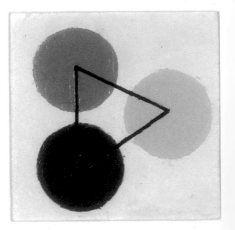

Reality exists in the city street. Illusion and imagination become ways to escape this often harsh reality. A homeless person's cardboard shanty rests against the granite permanence of an entry stair; mounds of discarded refuse obscure the edge dividing roadway and walk. The society matron's haute-couture dress shares an outdoor café with the hip-hopper's baggy pants and backward baseball cap. Garish graffiti whorls alternate with the ordered graphics of theater posters, their layers merging in an illustrated text of turf and control.

Streets are the main arteries of the city and the public heart of the neighborhood. The architecture of the buildings and the bordering facades interweave, giving the neighborhood its character. The cluttered wares of sidewalk vendors, the pristine displays in shop windows, and the unremitting flash of neon set the stage. Although the palette may change, this semblance of a bazaar stretches back to early times.

One of my early retail designs was instrumental in shaping the character of a street. The ornately detailed Victorian houses on San Francisco's Union Street provided an intimate setting for a boutique shopping complex at the foot of Pacific Heights.

Three empty, sagging, deteriorating houses still possessed detailing of Gothic inspiration. *(See* Union Street Stores *on pages 52 to 55.)*

Neighborhood commercial zoning instituted in the 1960s exempted renovation projects from the requirement of providing on-site parking. This fostered the then unusual idea of restoring old buildings instead of demolishing them.

To preserve these historic buildings, I elevated the existing buildings and added a floor beneath. I introduced glass shop windows on the lower level that merge with the historic appearance of the three houses. Restoring these Victorians with their gingerbread cornices and fish-scale clapboards, with the addition of found wrought-iron railings and gaslights, captured the image of San Francisco's romantic past. Stepping into the designer boutiques and intimate bistros, one senses the ambiance of a time when waistcoated merchants knew customers' names, small shops carried one-of-a-kind merchandise, and ladies with hand-painted parasols met top-hatted gentlemen for a leisurely afternoon tea.

The commercial success of the Union Street stores prompted others to follow its example. New interpretations of these design images spread up and down the street. While the individual designs were produced by many artists, designers, and architects, the Union Street shopping area is experienced as a whole—as a dynamic visual interplay of socioeconomic forces.

For each person, the mention of a particular city evokes memories of places experienced or images of places yet to be explored. Attitudes toward cities are as divergent as people's experiences of them. One person remembers a dinner by candlelight in a bistro, the festivity of a Thanksgiving Day parade, and an equestrian statue sharing a square with hordes of hungry pigeons. Another remembers the drunk sprawling in the gutter, the jostling of a crowd in a noontime rush, and the blaring horns of a bumper-to-bumper traffic jam. When people are asked to describe a specific city, more often than not they describe their experiences of that city. The images of the theatergoer and the tenement dweller are not congruent, yet both are true.

Just as nature connects its elements in a network rather than a chain, form interconnects in a four-dimensional whole. The dialogue between spontaneity and predictability, the temporary and the

— HILTON KRAMER • *Nature is a revelation of God; Art a revelation of man.* — HENRY WADSWORTH LONGFELLOW • *Men are wise*

FACING PAGE:
(above) Stairwell. (below) TRANSFORMA-
TION TRIPTYCH V. Oil on masonite. 6"x6".
Collection of the artist.

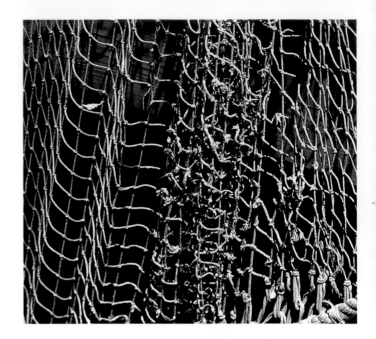

FACING PAGE:
Window detail.

in proportion, not to their experience, but to their capacity for experience. — GEORGE BERNARD SHAW • *You cannot depend on y*

UNION STREET STORES

These renovated Victorian houses with their gingerbread cornices, fish-scale clapboards, wrought-iron railings, and gaslights capture the image of San Francisco's romantic past. Stepping into the designer boutiques and intimate bistros, one senses the ambience of a time when waistcoated merchants knew their customers' names, small shops carried one-of-a-kind merchandise, and ladies with hand-painted parasols met top-hatted gentlemen for a leisurely afternoon tea.

when your imagination is out of focus. —MARK TWAIN • *Chaos, chance, order, harmony, and proportion all exist in human life,*

jewelry crafts

nature, and the finest art. — BEVERLY WILLIS • *The merit of originality is not novelty; it is sincerity.*— THOMAS CARLYLE • *Archite*

ats Man. Literature tells you about him. Painting will picture him to you. You can listen and hear him. But if you want to realize

(above, left) Street view of shops. (above, right) View before renovation. (below, right) Elevation.

permanent, evinces an energy that can never be adequately represented as a linear sum of its parts. The temporary, ethereal context and the permanent physical object are inseparable, demarcating a finite point within the infinity of time.

For example, as the Gold Rush boom town of San Francisco grew, the early urban-block grid pattern was simply extended, ignoring the forms of the hills. This made extremely steep slopes up and down the hills. The roar of cars climbing the steep grade of Nob Hill stirred the air, filling it with noise, pollution, and dirt, providing the sensory context for the Nob Hill Court condominiums. Townhouses and two- and three-story apartment buildings intermingled along Pine Street. Trademark San Francisco Bay windows lined the sidewalk edge, like the sheer cliffs of a plateau.

Reminded of immutable, impenetrable metamorphic rock cliffs and canyons, I "saw" a brick, wood, and cedar-shake-covered building, like cedar cliffs, cleft with transparent glass. The imperative here was to shield the inhabitant from the intrusion of the traffic demons. Concealed and surrounded within the privacy of the burnt-sienna and dove-gray clifflike

walls, the violated senses could find a quiet haven, safe and comfortable. Protecting walls contain a private, outdoor garden patio, free from traffic noise and pollution. *(See* Nob Hill Court Apartments *on pages 57 to 59.)*

To paint a mountain, the Renaissance artist found a hand-size rock fragment that possessed the images of peaks, valleys, and craggy cliffs. As a young artist, I found such a rock. In my Manhattan studio today, I will pick it up from my tool drawer, and my memory travels to mountains I have visited.

The invisible images evoked by visible form provide the senses with means to imagine an other, whatever it may be. In Eugene O'Neill's play *The Long Voyage Home* a young Swedish sailor returns to his mother and family farm after years at sea. José Quintero, director of a 1996 Broadway production, asked his actors to consider the sailor's main drive. "It is home." he said, "Home. This is where your heart has always been. Home. No more pain, no more loneliness. No more crying. You are going home."

him and experience him, go into his buildings. That is where you'll find him as he is. He can't hide there from you and he can't

om himself. — FRANK LLOYD WRIGHT • *Let our souls be mountains, Let our spirits be stars, Let our hearts be worlds.* — GAELIC

NOB HILL COURT APARTMENTS

Like the metamorphic rock of cliffs and canyons, the brick, wood, and cedar shakes of the Nob Hill Court apartments fuse to create a new form. These cedar cliffs, cleft with transparent glass, shield inhabitants from wind, rain, and intrusion. Concealed within these burnt-sienna, driftwood gray, and doe-skin walls is a secret haven, a safe and secure landscape garden.

MANTRA OF ORIGIN GIVEN TO ANSEL ADAMS • *I thought of medieval cities and the protective wall surrounding the inhabitants — i*

(above) Street view. (right) Elevation.

TIME

... Nature and time etch the wood surface's crevices just as they turn the smooth surface of tree trunks into rough bark. As leaves and blades of grass shrink and wither brown with age, wood shingles turn gray in salt-laden sea air or dark black-brown in fog.
I saw this building clad in shingles, imagining its character changing as time etched its crevices, aging it like a beautiful face.

the idea of an inhabited wall grew. — BEVERLY WILLIS • *Any man more right than his neighbors constitutes a majority of one.* —

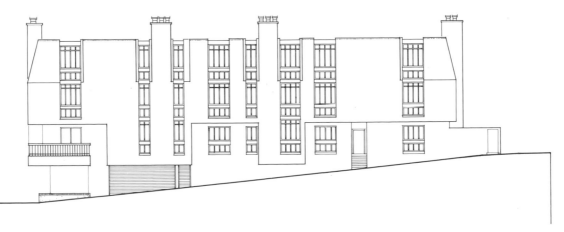

As natural elements recurred with some degree of regularity throughout history, man began to abstract their essential characteristics. The sun and moon were idealized in the circle, which, in turn, symbolized the cosmic wholeness of the psyche. The cardinal orientation points were idealized in the square, which in turn symbolized the physical world of body and matter. Thus a dialogue began between forms found in nature, such as the circle, and forms produced by humans.

Early civilizations believed that the harmony inherent in geometry was a metaphysical pattern that determined the physical nature of all things. The interpretation of geometry in terms of numeric relationships is a later intellectual rationalization of a natural system for the division of space.

As the natural world has been shown to operate according to certain mathematical "laws," it is easy to forget that mathematics—like art—exists primarily as a means of expressing fundamental relationships within the natural world. Nature does not obey mathematical law; mathematics merely attempts to describe nature through symbolic notation.

The very conception of geometric form is rooted in subjective interpretations of nature. The logarithmic spiral of the classic golden section can be found in the fossilized remains of a nautilus shell; a square or pentagon in the cross-section of a pepper; cubes in crystals of pyrite. Geometric shapes idealize the natural, smoothing away the dissimilar quirks of nature to find the common essence.

One day at the University of Hawaii, where I studied art, artist Professor Jean Charlot sent the class into a field to collect various flowers, pods, leaves, and stems and to look at nature's designs. The wondrous, endless forms and patterns of nature are readily apparent, merely waiting to be discovered and rediscovered. This experience inspired the design of the Leaf Table, commissioned by the Kailiani Hotel. Nature and geometry are intertwined. *(See* Leaf Table *on this page, lower right.)*

The Renaissance search for earthly realities added a third element, the figure of man. In *Vitruvian Man,* Leonardo da Vinci placed the male figure within both circle and square. There, man is represented as being at the center of creation, occupying both the irrational world of nature and the rational world of humanity.

Francesco di Giorgio Martini, another Renaissance theorist, used the human torso at the center of the circle and square to generate a planning system for cathedral design. His drawing of "cathedral man" is fully congruent with Michelangelo's floor plan at St. Peter's in Rome, the ancient mandala centered on the heart of the church where the nave and transept cross. *(See di Giorgio Martini's* Cathedral Man *on this page, lower left.)*

My proposed design for the Shown Winery in California's Napa Valley creates a dialogue between the asymmetrical forms of nature and the symmetrical forms of geometry, set against a backdrop of images derived from traditional wine making. The main building dominates the site, an invisible image of an old wooden cask, evident in its redwood staves and hoops of banded steel. The perfectly segmented geometry of the roof breaks at the building entrance, like a petal fallen from a flower.

Wine casks are best kept underground where the temperature and humidity are constant. The early Napa Valley vintners built their wineries close to the limestone ridges where they tunneled storage caves. The Shown Winery was planned for the flat ground of the valley floor. To make storage caves next to the building, I appropriated giant corrugated metal tubes used for

HENRY DAVID THOREAU • *The artist does not illustrate science [but] he frequently responds to the same interests that a scientist de*

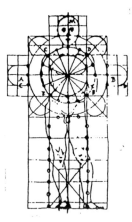

THIS PAGE:
(left) VITRUVIAN MAN superimposed on a cathedral plan (after di Georgio's model).
(right) LEAF TABLE TOP, 1957. Ceramic, 24" diameter. Sheraton Princess Kailani Hotel, Honolulu, Hawaii

FACING PAGE:
Shown Winery model.

NEXT SPREAD:
Shown Winery presentation drawings.

MUMFORD • *By taking a wedge from the circle or cylinder form, rupturing its closure, I symbolically questioned whether the idea*

of perfection is achievable. — BEVERLY WILLIS • *The true ideal is not opposed to the real but lies in it; and blessed are the*

it. — JAMES RUSSELL LOWELL • *Ideals are like the stars: we never reach them, but like the mariners of the sea, we chart our*

IMPERFECTION

... Shaped by nature's hand, the circular form of a daisy is marred by one shortened petal. The architect's circle is perfectly drawn by compass without flaw. For Plato, the circle was a symbol of universe: an ancient symbol of perfection. I lowered a section of a circular roof, receded a section of a circular wall to make an imperfect cylinder—like a natural flower made of wood and metal.

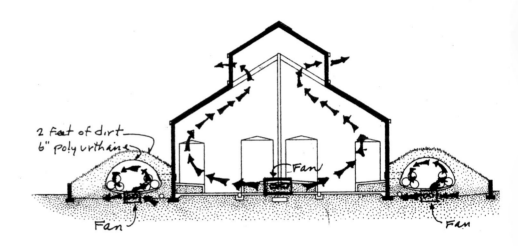

course by them. — CARL SCHURZ • *All art is a revolt against man's fate.* — ANDRÉ MALRAUX • *Nothing happen unless fir*

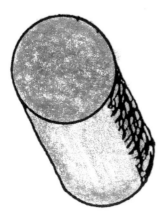

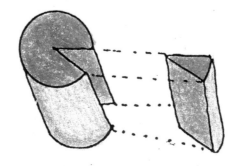

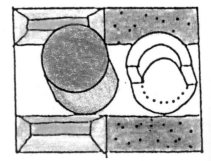

drainage culverts under highways. I calculated their passive energy requirements, covered them in polyurethane and earth, and proposed planting ground cover over the earthen berms. An access door to the cave was located at one end.

As the valley air cools to 50 degrees Fahrenheit at night, a small intake fan could cool the cave air to keep it a constant temperature suitable for aging wine. A similar process was used to keep the winery building cooled. In the winery, vents at the rooftop walls allowed the hot air to escape as the cool air entered. *(See* Shown Winery *on pages 61 to 64.)*

Outside the building entry and adjacent to the caves is a circular wine-tasting area. The plans of the wine-tasting terrace and the winery proper share a circular geometry yet remain as dissimilar as two individual snowflakes. Are the forms perfect or imperfect? Symmetrical or asymmetrical?

Awesomely beautiful and terrifyingly destructive, nature has engaged humanity in a tug-of-war between the desires to integrate and to dominate. Many twentieth-century artworks explore the complementary—and often contradictory —relationship between the organic shapes and materials generated by the earth and the more structured shapes and materials constructed by mankind.

The organic and man-made qualities stand out in architecture, which is of and with the land while exploiting technology and tradition. Frank Lloyd Wright's Falling-water appears to be both a part of nature and a fully man-made form. A rough stone core—a trace of the ancient *axis mundi*—rises vertically from a hearth formed by the rock outcropping of a waterfall. Cantilevered terraces, their engineering pushed to a seemingly magical limit, echo the horizontal landscape. The materials and textures come from nature; the shapes and structures from man. The resulting tension between organic and constructed, vertical and horizontal evokes the power of the Gothic cathedral.

At River Run, I played with the same double-sided archetype. A private residence and functioning vineyard nestled in the Napa Valley, the house is constructed like a rock of wood emerging from a tree-covered plateau and dwarfed by the mountains beyond. Natural materials and weathered textures are juxtaposed with formal geometry and crisp detail to suggest both rustic farmhouse and Palladian villa. The form echoes the natural landscape yet commands the valley beyond. Is it comfortable gentility or refined aristocracy? Farm or villa? Natural or constructed? *(See* River Run *on pages 66 to 73.)*

Within the panoply of interior forms shaped by sloped and flat ceilings of varying heights are views of outdoor vistas in each direction. These views, coupled with different room volumes, alter the indoor space like the patterns of a turning kaleidoscope.

Molded to the hilltop, covered in the rough bark of cedar shakes, the manor farm-house of the working vineyard below stands among the trees on the gently sloping knoll. Images of old Tuscany float through the casual viewer's mind, as the eye catches a glimpse of the perfectly balanced portico and arched windows. Seemingly endless rows of grapevines form a variegated green carpet on the surrounding valley floor.

1. — CARL SANDBURG • *Art is an effort to create, besides the real world, a more human world.* — ANDRÉ MAUROIS • *What*

SHOWN WINERY

Drifting gently downward are petal-like segments of a winery's round roof, not yet built. The redwood siding and steel bands that form the building's outside walls are like the oak staves and metal hoops of a wooden cask. On the wine-tasting terrace, a circular arbor awaits the fullness of the traditionally made wines fermented from the ripening grapes.

FACING PAGE:
(above) Airflow study. (below, left to right)
Forms study.

we need most is not so much to realize the ideal as to idealize the real. — H. F. HEDGE • *Whether man is disposed to yield to*

pose her, he cannot do without a correct understanding of her language. — JEAN ROSTAND • *The ignorant man marvels at the*

exceptional; the wise man marvels at the common; the greatest wonder of all is the regularity of nature. — GEORGE DANA BOARD

RIVER RUN RESIDENCE

Covered in a rough bark of cedar shakes, the manor house of a working vineyard stands among the trees on a gently sloping knoll. Images of old Tuscany float through the mind, as the eye catches a glimpse of the perfectly balanced portico, arched window, and seemingly endless rows of grapevines that form a green carpet on the surrounding valley floor.

PREVIOUS SPREAD:
Panoramic view of River Run.

THIS SPREAD:
Reflecting pool at night.

rmhouse is a study of contrasts, an assemblage of cultural ideas, a reflection of empirical and intellectual memories. — BEVERLY

WILLIS • *Indeed, all things must follow the demand of the principle of organic order.* — ELIEL SAARINEN • *The course of nature is the a*

THIS SPREAD:
Bathroom interior.

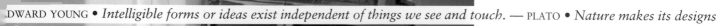

DWARD YOUNG • *Intelligible forms or ideas exist independent of things we see and touch.* — PLATO • *Nature makes its designs*

through the tenets of order. Nature does not know how beautiful the sunset is. — LOUIS KAHN • *Nay, nature's laws—the laws*

THIS PAGE:
(above, left) Scallop shell. (below, left) Rippling water. (above, right) Window detail.

FACING PAGE:
View of house from the pool.

SHELL

... Time's sea-born companion, the shell, is like an evolutionary womb filled with inherited memories of the restless, roaring sea and cresting waves. The shell's elegant shape—formed by its watery habitat—is arched and ribbed. Its splines thrust and reach outward from its base of alternating semicircular rings in variegated colors of growth. Its color, shape, and texture fascinate me. Inspired by a love for the shell's shape, I saw in its form the arch of the window with its thrusting mullions.

uty," if you will—are fundamental, and cannot be shaken by mere aesthetic conceitedness. — ELIEL SAARINEN • *Nature does not*

The German philosopher Martin Heidegger, in his essay "Discourse on Thinking," discusses the subject of *presence*: "The field of vision is something open, but its openness is not due to our looking." For Heidegger, the present—the now—is not a measurable unit of time but the result of presence, of the existent actively presenting itself. Heidegger's discourse explored the sense of thought. The invisible image, as a presence, affects thought, which in turn communicates to the senses experiences or feelings about space and place, form and texture, color and detail.

The devices of my designs—the utilization of that which is embodied in the feminine and masculine, the sacred and profane, the illusion and reality, the myth and narrative—are ways to communicate. While these means can be used to convey cold, harsh realities and prisonlike environments, I choose to use them to achieve balance, serenity, harmony, and spatial warmth. Presence cannot be photographed, only experienced.

Industrial designers Charles and Ray Eames, Raymond Loewy, and Henry Dreyfuss theorized that design is a means to communicate commercially. Through their work they demonstrated that design could motivate people to buy a product. Certain designs sold. Many of these designs are now museum pieces. I was fascinated by the visual power of design to create a desire to possess. This is the result of presence of the existent actively presenting itself, as Heidegger suggested—a thought created by design, which actively motivates desire.

However, in the mid-sixties, the typical retailer was still not convinced that design sold. Through a chance encounter, I met a person who wanted to open a store. We decided do it together. What an opportunity to test the idea that interior design could also sell products! We named the store, located near the Union Street stores, "Capricorn." I created an interior in an image of the countryside— with unfinished barn walls, old brick, refurbished pine furniture, ice boxes, and hutches. I covered the painted concrete floor with sawdust. Unfinished, used nail barrels and wood shelves—not typical aluminum ones—displayed French and Italian cookware and kitchen accessories. This was a dramatic contrast to the fifties-style aluminum, glass, and colored-ceramic tile storefronts. The shop was an immediate financial success. I had empirical evidence of my design's ability to affect behavior.

A concurrent marketing question was how to create a desire for the density and constraints of multifamily housing in the minds of Californians accustomed to single-family living. (The undeveloped land itself was more suited to conventional one-acre lots.) Marketing ideas included club houses, children's play yards, freedom from maintenance chores, and—in the Pacific Point condominium homes—the added pleasure of views. But presence—the existent actively presenting itself—was to be found in the invisible images that connect design and nature.

Chinese *Kanyu*—or *feng shui*— is rooted in both Confucian and Taoist principles. (Confucians believe that a person's life is governed by fate, geomancy, virtue, education, experience, exposure, upbringing, cultural and social contacts, and actions. The Taoists believe that patience, harmony, simplicity, and contentment are the keys to human coexistence with nature.) The effect of natural forces upon manmade structures, on the earth's energy, their relationship to the heavens; the understanding of each land form's unique topographic and geographic characteristics; the influences of the physical environment; and the cycle of changes are applied to

complete things. She is chaotic. Man must finish, and he does so by making a garden and building a wall. — ROBERT FROST • *We*

Transformation Triptych
Exploration

Three views of infinite space (blank field), identities, forces, and enclosures exploring potential relations.

...member that what we observe is not nature in itself, but nature exposed to our method of questioning. — WERNER HEISENBERG •

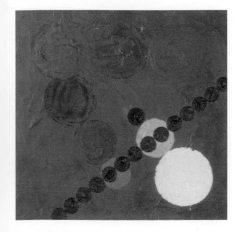

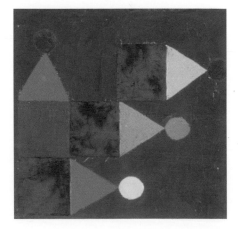

Even if each building is the same design, differences in individual building facades, siting, and access provide an overall appearan

PACIFIC POINT CONDOMINIUMS

Slicing through apartment facades, wall planes fan out in space, their subtle shifts directing the eye toward a breathtaking view of the Pacific Ocean. Whether slowly walking along the promenade or sitting on a private balcony, one hears the roaring surf pound nature's changing rhythms on the shell-strewn beach—a symphony of sight and sound intermittently muted by enfolding fog.

each building's orientation, concentrating on achieving maximum comfort and a conducive human environment.

A thread seems to connect not only designer, observer, form, and event but observers in all times. I believe the emotive content of design transcends cultural, political, economic, and linguistic barriers. Developers of the first large-scale communities on hills ignored the delicate balance of nature, its form and ecosystems. Rampant bulldozing upset balances so carefully wrought by nature. Nature retaliated with flooding, mud slides, and blights. Prior to the design of Pacific Point condominiums, I wanted to be thoroughly knowledgeable of the site's ecosystem. Traditional architectural tools were inadequate for the magnitude of the necessary analytical tasks. Consequently, my associates and I found computer programs that we could apply or readapt to serve our purposes for site analysis and planning. Originally developed during World War II, some programs were converted for industrial use by oil companies and archived at Kansas State University Geological School. These map-plotting programs could draw topographic maps, drainage diagrams, and soil-movement patterns and calculate earth

removal. We made matrices from existing geological research, which allowed us to evaluate potential areas of significant environmental impact, causal relationships, and specific areas of eco-sensitivity. They were also used for a combined eco-socioeconomic analysis of each proposed plan.

An associate, Jochen Eigen, wrote a series of computer programs that tested the compatibility of a proposed floor plan to the site conditions in conjunction with the plotting programs. I named this system CARLA (Computerized Approach to Residential Land Analysis).

With these tools I carefully planned stepped terraces on the bluff side of the site downward toward the ocean and designed a bridgelike entry to the three-story building's mid-section. My design used diagonally placed interior walls that slice through the apartment facades, elongating one side like a fan. These subtle diagonal wall planes direct the eye to a breathtaking view of the Pacific Ocean. Walking the winding path down the stepped slopes, sitting on the coastal rocks, or watching from the balcony, one feels nature's pounding rhythms on the shell-strewn beach and the roaring surf beyond: a symphony of sight and sound,

intermittently muted by the enfolding fog. For the occupants the buildings are symbiotically juxtaposed to their natural surroundings. *(See* Pacific Point Condominiums *on pages 75 to 76.)*

Our work with computers led to a commission to design a prototypical computer building for the Internal Revenue Service. Unfortunately, President Jimmy Carter vetoed the appropriations for the building. Bowing to public concerns about the computer, he sought to block the automation of the income tax form. Notwithstanding the lack of funds, automation marched on, and every tax return eventually became computerized. Unfortunately, the building remains unbuilt.

Carter thought his veto would protect the public from an invasion of privacy, but actually many individual returns were already computerized. The existing nine IRS regional processing centers were rectangular in shape, each the size of a football field, one story with low ceilings, fluorescent lights, and no partitions. Inside, row upon row of computer desks were lined up, classroom style. The General Service Administration sought to alleviate this grim, barren environment by connecting it to my new, taller, hexagonal

l variety. — BEVERLY WILLIS • *Realization is sensing the harmony of systems. It is the sense of order, or one may say that order is*

building, filled with natural light.

The prismatic Computer Center fit the nine different existing building configurations. An interior atrium was meant to be like the core of a geode, bouncing shafts of daylight throughout the interiors. The form and detail allow the individual and machine to interact serenely and efficiently. Functionally, the Computer Center was supposed to receive, store, and automatically process the truckloads of computer disks submitted by large corporations in lieu of paper printouts. *(See* Internal Revenue Service Computer Center *on pages 79 to 82.)*

Leonardo da Vinci—who conceived airplanes centuries before they existed—would have been mystified by the images that are conjured up on computer screens. Leonardo's world was mechanically based. The electronic world would have seemed terrifying: a product of witchcraft or sorcery. No known experience could have explained such images or connected them with reality.

But technical competence—even technical brilliance—has never been sufficient to create a masterpiece. Transcending the specifics of time and place, masterpieces are illuminated not by the light without, but by the light within—by the invisible forces radiating from human desire and experience. Empathetic communication, not technical objectification, defines these works. Their silent language becomes the personal thread that draws the individual into the ever-evolving tapestry of shared experience.

the name given to a harmony of systems. — LOUIS KAHN • To *fit the nine different sites with their different building configuration*

FACING PAGE:
(above) Floor plan for the IRS Computer Center. (below) TRANSFORMATION TRIPTYCH. Oil on masonite. 6"x6". Collection of the artist.

Transformation Triptych

Changeling

An identity (circle) is affected by two different types of forces (triangles), losing its original identity, changing into two different entities (circles of different dimensions).

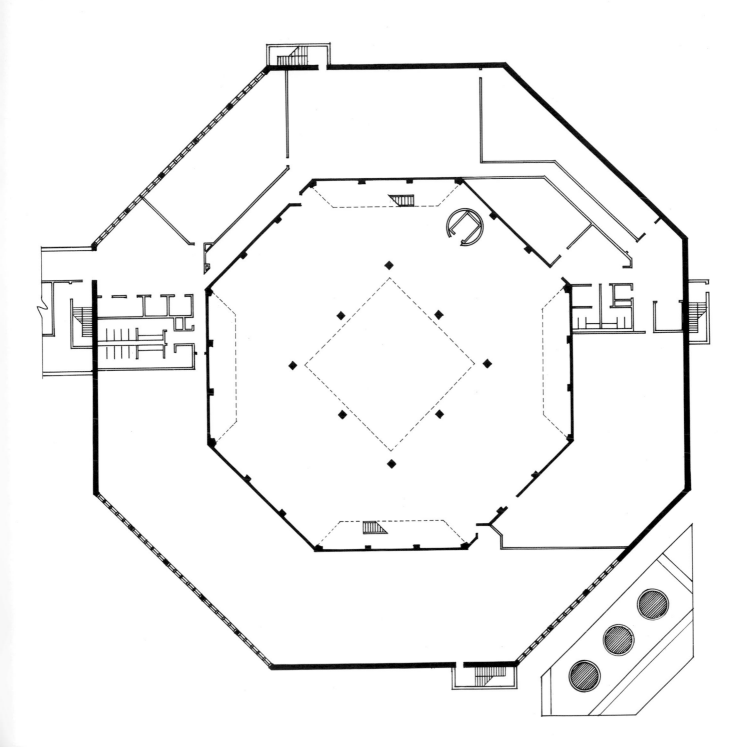

ding was to be linked to the "mother" building through an umbilical-cord-like passage. — BEVERLY WILLIS • *Art, like morality,*

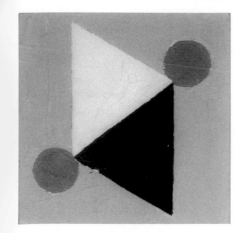
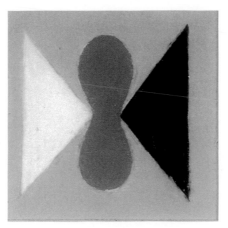
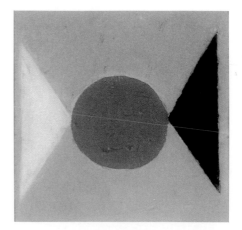

consists in drawing the line somewhere. — GILBERT K. CHESTERTON • *Nature is an endless thread weaving eternally.* — BEVERLY W

IRS COMPUTER CENTER

Secure yet flexible, the prismatic shape of a
proposed prototypical computer center
locks into multiple building configurations.
An interior court becomes the jewel-like
core of a geode, bouncing shafts of daylight
throughout the center's interior. Housing a
glittering diamond of technology, the form
allows the individual and machine to interact
quietly and efficiently.

tension between the technological and the natural is the root conflict of our culture. — LEO MARX • *The art that is coming will*

(above, left) Butte. (above, right) Model for the
IRS Computer Center.

MOUNTAIN STRONG

... I saw the mass of the building like that of the mountain, solid and strong. Its ridges and crevices are like battle scars: mute testimony to its ancient bouts with storms and fire. Its form inspires design; its resiliency is a model for construction. The building, like the mountain, feels permanent: a bulwark against natural disasters, a shelter from sun, cold, wind, and rain.

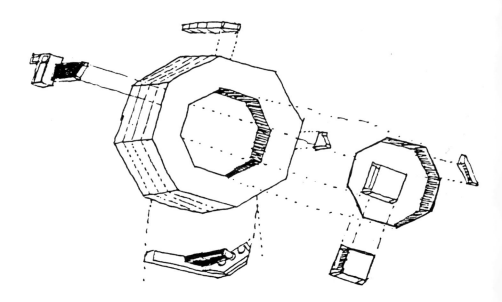

give formal expression to our scientific conviction. — FRANZ MARC • *Every artist dips his brush in his own soul, and paints his*

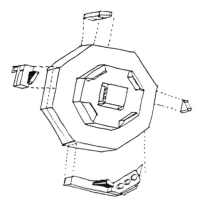

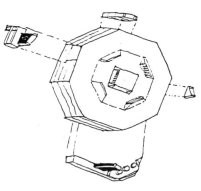

THIS PAGE:
Exploded isonometrics.

The eye sees an object or specific form as both differentiated from and intertwined with its environment. The simultaneous grasp of figure and ground, object and context, affords meaning. Thus, one determines whether a cross is an object of religious significance, an arithmetical notation, or a pattern of bars forming a cage. In like manner, one discerns whether an arch connotes an entrance to a church or the availability of fast food.

In this manner the image of the street and buildings are "read" by the people in them. Our early ancestors read every broken twig, crushed leaf, footprint, or sudden movement. Survival depended upon this skill. Contemporary citizens instinctively read the faces, body movements, and clothes of passersby. Watchful eyes glance quickly to evaluate potentially dangerous conditions. Children are taught to be fearful of strangers. The same intuitive sense that guided cave dwellers tells us whether strangers are friendly or threatening, approachable or insular, respectful or repudiating.

The individual reads the socioeconomic status of the people who live on a street by observing well-maintained facades, clean, well-lit, tree-lined boulevards, or barren pavements lined with deteriorating buildings, graffiti, broken concrete sidewalks, and litter. The first communicates the prosperity of its inhabitants, the second their poverty.

Whether intuitive or learned, these images are instantly interpreted. People who live on the landscaped street in a good neighborhood lined with expensive homes usually receive adequate city services, like police protection, clean, well-maintained streets with regular garbage pick-up, prompt newspaper deliveries and mail service, and quick repair of telephone, gas, and electric lines.

At the other extreme are the poorer neighborhoods, which often seem abandoned. Refuse collects on the sidewalks and in the gutters, streets are filled with potholes, repair barricades seem to stay in place for months. The inhabitants expect and are accustomed to little and suffer the gangs that band lawlessly together, that prey on the innocent and helpless, like wild animals.

The Children's Recreational Center in Margaret Hayward Park, San Francisco, was located in such a neighborhood until the redevelopment agency built new townhouses with fenced yards. But a forbidding chain-link metal fence remained around the park, which the authorities thought would mediate between neighborhood violence and the innocence of children at play. Located in the corner of the park behind the tennis courts, the play area was situated next to a small structure that previously served as a community room—adjacent to the open park space reserved for informal football and baseball games. The original neoclassical building's formal access was also compromised when the intimidating fencing was installed.

Children are quick to read imagery. A child learns from a parent's frown, particular sounds, tones of voice, or body movements, even before he or she knows right from wrong or good from bad. Since children could read the building's body language, the design needed to be welcoming and suggestive of fun and play, and appeal to the imagination. It is also needed to be sensitively scaled to fit a child's size. As an artist years earlier, I had painted a fresco in Honolulu for Palama Settlement—a community center for disadvantaged children. The fresco narrated how an empathic counselor led the children away from dangerous participation in street gang brawls and introduced them to theatrical roles in which they could be warriors in their own imaginations. Thus, they could dissipate their anger in a nonviolent way.

ure into his pictures. — HENRY WARD BEECHER • *I tried to see space, material, and artifact through children's eyes to provide a*

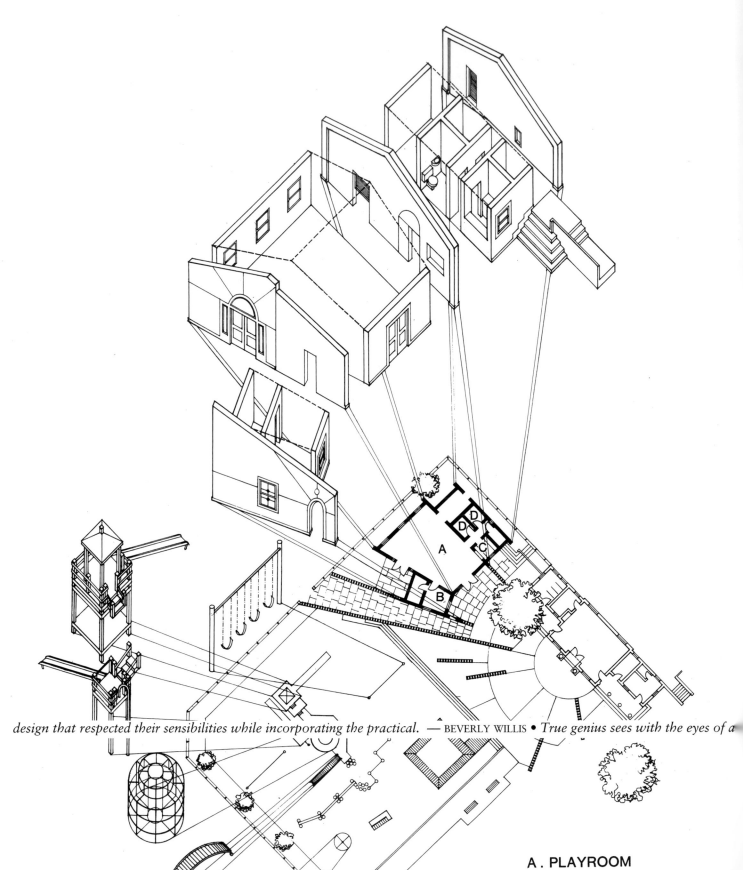

design that respected their sensibilities while incorporating the practical. — BEVERLY WILLIS • *True genius sees with the eyes of a*

A . PLAYROOM
B . OFFICE
C . KITCHEN
D . RESTROOM

CIRCLES

... The sun circles and gives way to the circular moon. The planets orbit and seasons rotate in a silent rhythm, ending in closure. Nature's circle is burnt into my memory, permeating philosophical ideas and each creative thought. It inspires symbols and the design of plans, columns, cupolas, and arches, all connecting architecture to nature's circular obsession.

inks with the brain of a genii. — PUZANT KEVORK THOMAHAN • *One of the advantages of being disorderly is that one is constant-*

FACING PAGE:
Exploded axonometric of the Margaret Hayward Center.

THIS PAGE:
Wall opening.

ly making exciting discoveries. — A. A. MILNE • Imagination disposes of everything; it creates beauty, justice, and happiness, whic

I designed the building to be lower in height than the tallest play equipment—like a toy building. The structure fans out of its tight corner site, and diagonal walls shift through the structure, like the joints of the armadillo shell. The facade stops at a wide walkway, bordered by three tiered steps. Together, these elements create an illusion of a stage platform. On the right wing "stage" wall, which extends past the building, I placed an arched opening that leads nowhere but beckons the young to pass through and explore. The painted arch opening and circular moon above are as magical as Alice's looking-glass, leading from everywhere to everywhere. (See Children's Recreational Center in Margaret Hayward Park on pages 84 to 89.)

Childhood is the time to find invisible images, to imagine and dream, to see something where nothing is apparent, and to begin to grasp myth, narrative, illusion, chaos, and inspiration.

I learned early on the powerful affect that design images exert on behavior. Among my first architectural commissions, I designed the interiors of military officers' clubs in Hawaii. Air Force Sergeant Johnny Moran, who ran the noncommissioned officers' club at Hickam Air Force Base, wanted a

club for his men like the officers' club, but the high command was adamantly opposed: it would be a misuse of funds to provide wood-paneled and wallpapered walls and upholstered furniture, paintings, and sculpture for the rowdy, noncommissioned officers who regularly broke the furniture in drunken brawls. Typical of the legendary supply sergeants of two world wars, nothing was impossible for the wily Moran. I was commissioned to design a structure of a quality equal to an officers' club. The change in the behavior of its members was astounding. The brawls completely ceased. Without rules or management suggestion, the members arrived neatly groomed and often brought their girlfriends or families: a drastic departure from their earlier dirty, slovenly appearance and foul-mouthed, rowdy behavior.

To attribute meaning to art and architecture, some point of access must exist between viewer and the architectural form, some experiential grounding to make personal understanding possible. Just as any spoken language is reduced to babble without common understanding of meaning, architecture is reduced to empty gestures when it fails to evoke a common experience. Consider for a moment the potential of

the silent languages that public schools typify in many urban areas. The architect and planner imagine the school as an oasis of opportunity in an otherwise barren, war-torn desert. The administrator and educator imagine the school as a final bastion against social disintegration and self-destruction. The school-as-fortress emerges complete with metal detectors, barred windows, bullet-proof glass, and security fences. What image comes into the mind of a student who gazes at this citadel of learning? A prison? Granite-faced and perhaps containing a multimedia computer center, but a prison nonetheless.

For the design team, the underlying images might be protective and intended to aid in developing the student's full potential within the institution. To the student, the images are likely to be of forced confinement, not of intellectual achievement. Bars and gates seem the neighborhood norm; academic excellence the exception. One can understand the negative message implied by present-day security systems and see the need to make images that communicate positive images of academic importance.

Unlike art, a building simultaneously serves a multiplicity of functional, socio-

thing in this world. — BLAISE PASCAL • *In every condition of humanity, it is precisely play, and play alone that makes man com-*

plete. — FRIEDRICH SCHILLER • *Thought is the blossom; language the bud; action the fruit behind it.*—RALPH WALDO EMERSON • *If*

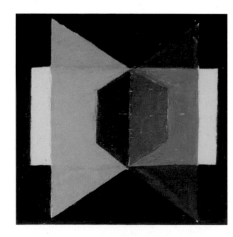
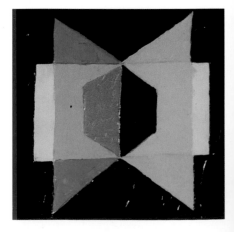

...nourish the roots of our culture, society must set the artist free to follow his vision wherever it takes him.— JOHN FITZGERALD

Transformation Triptych
Spatial

Two spaces (blank fields) float in an outer space (field). Rotating, the inner and outer spaces penetrate each other, changing their tone (color).

FACING PAGE:
(above) Play area. (below) TRANSFORMA-
TION TRIPTYCH. Oil on masonite. 6"x6".
Collection of the artist.

THIS PAGE:
(above, left) Moon. (middle, left) Beach.
(below, left) Wall opening detail. (above, right)
Detail from wall to roof.

MARGARET HAYWARD CENTER

In a recreational center for children, an arched opening crowned by a painted full-moon-like circle seems as magical as Alice's looking-glass, leading from everywhere to everywhere and beckoning the young to pass through and explore. Wide outdoor steps become a tiered stage; the opening invites childhood dreams of stardom. Lower in height than the playground climbing tower, the building is the children's treasured playhouse.

KENNEDY • *No culture can live, if it attempts to be exclusive.*— MAHATMA GANDHI • *That is true culture which helps us*

(above, left) Exterior of the Manhattan Village Academy.
(above, right) Front entry and stairs to first floor.

MANHATTAN VILLAGE ACADEMY

This small reform-minded high school for 350 public school students is set in a loft space located in an art nouveau-style tall building in New York's Chelsea district. Its welcoming environment communicates positive images of academic importance and serves a number of functional, sociological, and psychological needs. The free-flowing, community-styled classroom space provides a relaxing, soothing atmosphere, conducive to both teaching and learning.

for the social betterment of all. — HENRY WARD BEECHER • *Culture is the habit of being pleased with the best and know-*

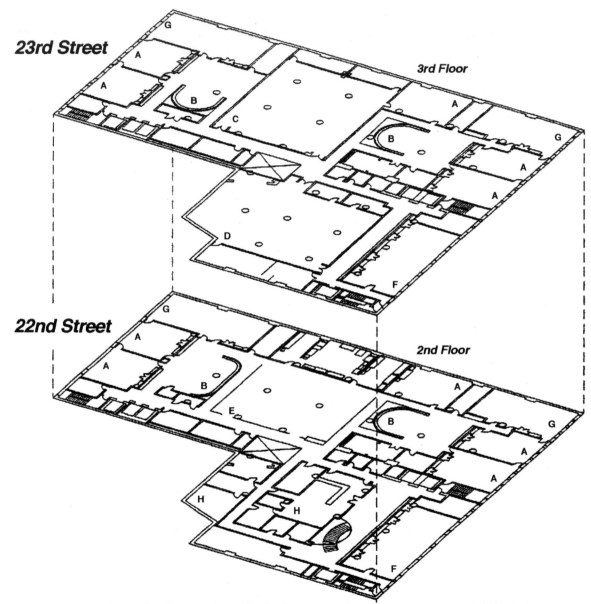

23rd Street

3rd Floor

22nd Street

2nd Floor

ing why.— HENRY VAN DYKE • *A work of art is that which elicits a prolonged suspension of disbelief.* — COLIN ROWE • *Re*

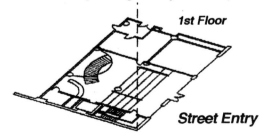

1st Floor

Street Entry

LOCUS PLAN
A. CLASSROOMS
B. QUAD
C. ASSEMBLY HALL
D. MEDIA CENTER/LIBRARY
E. CAFETERIA
F. ART ROOM
G. SCIENCE/MATH ROOM
H. ADMINISTRATION

he right of self-respect breeds respect. — BEVERLY WILLIS • *The building's environment must support the building of the*

STUDENTS

... like a new-born flower unfolding, breaking new ground, blooming in supportive soil, learning builds within. Teaching plants hope, supports dreams, cultivates strength to be independent. I remembered the echo of the barren, functional, institutional halls, cold-barred windows, and chain-linked stairwells, building symbols of the ugliness, of poverty, storms of rage, the agony of despair. I sought a design that would communicate the dignity and importance of education, touched by caring and respect—a plan of open, quiet, free-flowing spaces with classrooms filled with the feeling of possible dreams.

FACING PAGE:
The Locus Plan.

THIS PAGE:
(top, left) Cross section of Glory-Bush fruit, Courtesy of Harvard Botanical Museum; (center, left) individual flowers on a common stem; and (bottom, left) a student in an art class. (top, right) Media Center and Library; (bottom, right) Students in an art and ceramic class.

93

mind. — BEVERLY WILLIS • *The eye sees contrast, the mind compares.* — BEVERLY WILLIS • *What is wanted is not the will to be*

(above) Interior quad.
(right) Math and science lab.

logical, and psychological needs.

Using design to encourage positive behavior was an important objective for Manhattan Village Academy High School. Its student body, like that of other New York City public schools, is multicultural. Its Caucasian population is less than 30 percent. In New York City the "chalk and talk" model plan with classrooms connected to lengthy, winding corridors did not fit the reform pedagogy of its sponsor, the Center for Collaborative Education, headed by Deborah Meier.

The reform pedagogy believes in teaching using projects that simultaneously develop a range of student learning and experiential skills. This requires a different floor plan, one that allows true flexibility of spatial configurations to fit the varying teaching needs of different types of individual and group projects while still facilitating standard lecture requirements.

Group images collide in the teaching and learning experience. Within each student are the buried memories and associations of home and street. In less affluent neighborhoods, the home and street communicate images of worthlessness, hopelessness, and defeat. Dreams of the future and self-fulfillment are often crushed, cre-

ating tension, anger, and instability. Minds and emotions filled with conflict, rebellion, and insecurity are difficult vessels for learning—posing incredible challenges for educators.

The invisible images of design affect thought, either exacerbating the explosive tensions dwelling within or soothing raging emotions. The soothing, serene environment of Manhattan Village Academy strengthens the effectiveness of the teaching discipline and its creative approaches. Its space allows students to lose themselves in projects, whether writing, publishing, and presenting a book; reading and making the sets and costumes for a Shakespearean play; or interpreting literature through play acting the roles of a book's characters.

Computers in each classroom and in the Media Center–Library are integral to learning and self-expression. Behind the computer screen lies a world of images— a world freed from physical, political, and economic constraints, a world beyond the apparent chaos of random access and gigabytes. Where invisible images can be made into virtual images. Where in the grassy greens and Caribbean blues of the wired metallic maze of a circuit board, an electronic metropolis can emerge: the towering

libraries of memory and the commercial buildings of multimedia cluster in neighborhood centers, surrounded by residences with their curving balconies and terraces. Where the mass-transit expressways and the locally routed streets of digital traces provide easy access for split-second communication. Behind the chaos of technology lies another order, a world humming with the energy of new life, one in which every student can participate. *(See Manhattan Village Academy on pages 91 to 93.)*

Who will write the new myths and create the new illusions within this new world? What sexual energy will be sparked, what new ideal discovered? And where, in this most profane of worlds, lies a new sacred essence waiting to be revealed?

Will the visible forms of the future be shaped by the language of digital technology or transformed by the silent language of art and architecture?

The answer depends on what one truly sees.

Beverly Willis

e wish to find out, which is the exact opposite. — BERTRAND RUSSELL • *We build statues out of snow, and weep to see them*

REFERENCES

Art through the Ages, 5th ed. Revised by Horst de la Croix and Richard Tansey (New York: Harcourt, Brace & World, 1970).

Alberti, Leon Battista. *The Ten Books of Architecture* (New York: Dover Publications, 1986).

Arnheim, Rudolf. *Visual Thinking* (Berkeley: University of California Press, 1969).

Arnheim, Rudolf. *Art and Visual Perception: A Psychology of the Creative Eye* (Berkeley: University of California Press, 1954).

Berger, John. *About Looking* (New York: Vintage International Edition, September 1991).

Le Corbusier. *The Modulor 1 & 2* (Cambridge: Harvard University Press, 1980).

Eliade, Mircea. *The Sacred and the Profane* (New York: Harcourt, Brace & World, 1959).

Eliot, Alexander. *Sight and Insight* (New York: McDowell, Obolensky, 1959).

The Encyclopedia of World Mythology. Foreword by Rex Warner (New York: Garland Books, 1975).

Freemason, Eugene S. "The Mind's Eye: Nonverbal Thought in Technology." *Science* 197, no. 4306 (August 26, 1977):

827–36.

Gleick, James. *Chaos: Making a New Science* (New York: Penguin Group/Viking Penguin, 1987).

Ghyka, Matila. *The Geometry of Art and Life* (New York: Dover Publications, 1977).

Heidegger, Martin. *Discourse on Thinking.* Translated by John Anderson and Hans Freund (New York: Harper & Row, 1966).

Huntley, H. E. *The Divine Proportion: A Study in Mathematical Beauty* (New York: Dover Publications, 1970).

Jung, Carl. *Man and His Symbols* (New York: Doubleday and Company, 1964).

Kandinsky, Wassily. *Point and Line to Plane* (New York: Dover Publications, 1977).

Lip, Evelyn. *Feng Shui: Environments of Power—A Study of Chinese Architecture* (London: Academy Editions, 1995).

McHarg, Ian L. *Design with Nature* (New York: John Wiley and Sons, 1992).

Morgan, Morris Hicky, Ph.D. *Marcus Vitruvius Pollio: The Ten Books on Architecture* (New York: Dover Publications, 1960), 104.

Norberg-Sculz, Christian. *Architecture:*

Meaning & Place Selected Essays (New York: Rizzoli International Publications, 1988).

Palladio, Andrea. *The Four Books of Architecture* (New York: Dover Publications, 1965).

Pennick, Nigel. *Sacred Geometry: Symbolism and Purpose in Religious Structures* (Wellingborough, Northamptonshire, England: Turnstone Press Limited, 1980).

Rasmussen, Steen Eiler. *Experiencing Architecture* (Cambridge: MIT Press, 1959).

Rundle, Clark R.T. *Myth and Symbol in Ancient Egypt* (London: Thames and Hudson, Limited, 1978).

Viollet-Le-Duc, Eugene Emmanuel. *Lectures on Architecture* (New York: Dover Publications, 1987).

Whitford, Frank. *Bauhaus* (New York: Thames and Hudson, Limited, 1984).

Wittkower, Rudolf. *Architectural Principles in the Age of Humanism* (London: Academy Editions, 1973).

melt. — SIR WALTER SCOTT • *Speak to the earth, and it shall teach thee.* — JOB 12:8 • *Conform and be dull.* — J. FRANK D

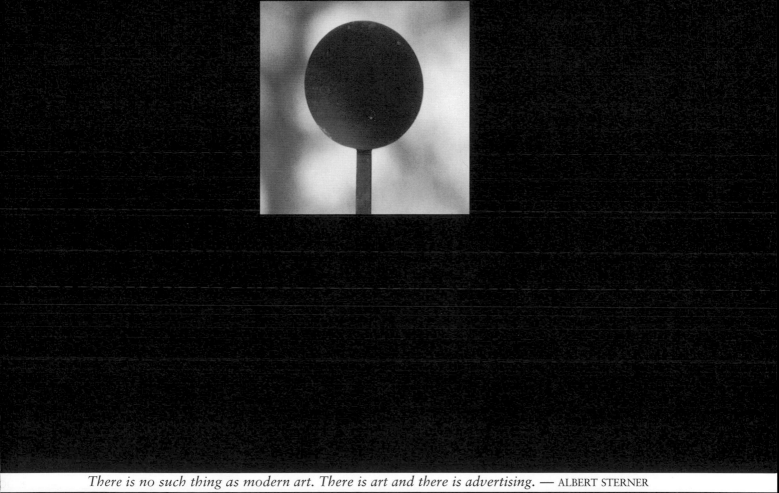

There is no such thing as modern art. There is art and there is advertising. — ALBERT STERNER

AN IMAGE OF BEVERLY WILLIS

On a cold day in 1932, a five-year-old tomboy climbed out of a truck from alongside her father. It was late at night, and they had just ended a twelve-hour drive back from the nearest town, carrying with them replacement machinery for a broken oil rig. In front of them, the road faded into the dust of an Oklahoma oil field. The barren earth, dotted with creaking steel machinery, was saturated with a thick oil film. In the darkness, circles of blackness gleamed under occasional spotlights.

Beverly Willis's life as an artist and architect begins here. Born in Tulsa, Oklahoma, in 1928 and weaned on these Midwestern oil fields, Willis experienced an America awestruck by the machine, nostalgic for the days of westward expansion, and determined to preserve its puritan ethic. From the landscape of oil fields and pioneer homesteads, and later from institutional homes, Willis was drawn into the world of building.

Willis became an architect in part to make sense of American rural ideals. Her architecture reveals none of the grand theoretical abstractions that dominated the work of the European avant-garde during her youth. Instead, it stems from rural pragmatism—from a desire to tackle the reality of life. The anguish of building, of clearing and shaping the land, coupled with attention to the forces that allow a project to come into being: the social factors and know-how that a working architect must assimilate.

Rooted in early images and myths, Willis was able to forge a path unique in a profession that still scorns the abilities of women builders. She has explored painting, industrial design, architecture, and urban planning. By the late seventies, at the zenith of her practice, she headed one of the few architectural firms in the country run by a woman, had several large-scale civic projects in the works, and had built herself an estate in the Napa Valley. In short, she found her voice.

Willis's father, Ralph William Willis, married Margaret Elizabeth Porter, a nurse, and founded the ambitiously named National Tool Company while still in his twenties. In doing so, he put an end to a long line of pioneers extending back to the early seventeenth century. His daughter never knew the pioneer life, but the image was deeply ingrained in her. Willis's paternal grandfather, Charles William Willis, had struggled to forge a community and tame the wilderness. The family lore glorified his experiences.

Charles William Willis built a fashionable mansion in Broken Bow, Nebraska, symbolizing the triumph of rural innocence and persistence. As a homesteader allotted a parcel of land under the federal government's Homestead Act in the boom years of westward expansion, Willis made his fortune pioneering. At the 1904 Saint Louis World's Fair, he found an impressive prototype of a Queen Anne-style house, which he took back with him to rural Nebraska.

The vast dwelling was firmly planted on a hill. Willis, together with his extended family, refashioned the raw property using trees gathered from his lands. With a gabled roof, sweeping porch, shingle cladding and erect demeanor, the house echoed another persistent image in the American collective unconscious: the castle on the hill with the pristine picket fence. Here everyone contributed to the work, and the images of home and creator fused: to live was to build.

The Broken Bow house was not only a victory over harsh elements but a model of how permanent connections to the land are forged. The young Beverly Willis took great pride in her connection to this symbolic structure. She yearned for such a

...hitecture is the most public of the arts. It surrounds us. It touches us continually. It is inescapable. It affects all of us, all of the

time. Its importance cannot be overstated.—JANE ALEXANDER • *The people who make art their business are mostly impostors.* —

home, an ideal that she experienced only through photographs. The stately mansion stood in strong contrast to the more brutal images of her own childhood landscapes.

The Oklahoma oil fields of Willis's own youth constitute another cultural layer, aggressively focused on an industrial future. Here life was most visible in the rigid, violent rhythms of the pumps that rocked back and forth twenty-four hours a day and the derricks that sometimes spouted without warning. Scattered haphazardly among the machinery, the workers' housing was, like everything else, temporary: wood-frame, one-story, shotgun-plan huts, covered with tar paper to protect inhabitants from the harsh climate.

There were few women around. The men, bound in a struggle with machines, worked around the clock according to the rhythms of the pumps. As they groped over the derricks, moving in and out of the darkness, Willis followed them. She was both attracted and disgusted by this landscape: the energy and tension contrasted with the horror of the soot and oil that stuck to her body.

It is tempting to see Willis's later career as an architect as a quest to rediscover the more pristine landscape of her grandfa-

ther's family, but both the genteel and the brutal images are equally romanticized. More importantly, both convinced Willis that the world could be shaped on any scale, by anyone. They are images of struggle against adversity: man struggling with the massive and relentless machine and an untamed natural landscape shaped by rural persistence and idealism.

Under the strains of the Great Depression, Ralph Willis's business foundered. In 1934, Willis's parents divorced. Willis and Ralph Gerald ("Budd") Willis, her only sibling, were taken from the oil fields and left in an orphanage. There, enclosed behind concrete-block institutional walls, they encountered a predictably oppressive world. The dreariness and the rigidity of the institution reinforced each other: the children were taught that the imagination was worthless. They were not encouraged to forge their own paths.

Willis pitted this image of a drab life under the crushing weight of unfeeling institutions against her early memories of rural life, even at its most violent. One could either overcome one's environment, as had the men in her youthful memories of the oil fields, or be destroyed by it. Willis rightfully credits the images of ruggedness that had

framed her childhood as allowing both her and her brother to establish a fierce—while resented—independence at the orphanage. In fact, these images liberated her curiosity and drove her to design.

The social changes that faced women with the advent of World War II fed this deeply imbedded sense of independence. Suddenly women had broader—if short-lived—opportunities. By the time Willis was seventeen, she had worked in a welding shop, learning to rivet, to wire equipment, and to practice woodworking. She dreamed of enlisting in the Woman's Air Corps and did learn to fly a plane, but she was too young and had to content herself with a pilot's license.

With the end of the war, Willis entered Oregon State University to study aeronautical engineering. She sensed, however, that the door of opportunity that had been opened briefly to women was beginning to close. Not satisfied with the path offered to women in the postwar period - marriage and motherhood - Willis was still searching for her calling. After two years, she withdrew from Oregon State and worked for a brief stint in a lithographer's studio. A year later she left for San Francisco.

San Francisco—the city that would one

so • *Culture is the widening of the mind and of the spirit.* — JAWAHARLAL NEHRU • *Behind changing natural form there lies pure*

day become the center of Willis's creative work—was at this point only another way station. She entered the San Francisco Art Institute, apprenticed as an actress, and built sets. Her art studies led to a one-woman show of watercolors at a local gallery, but Willis did not find sufficient opportunities to test her skills. Prodded by two Chinese artist friends who saw connections between her paintings and Asian art, Willis drifted further west to Hawaii.

For Willis, Hawaii relentlessly fueled the exhilaration that comes with making things. Perhaps the calm isolation of island life gave her a first taste of rootedness. Willis quickly inserted herself in the island culture and made Hawaii her home. She studied fresco painting under Jean Charlot at the University of Hawaii, graduating in 1954 with a Bachelor of Fine Art. She continued to paint and began to explore abstract techniques, such as those practiced by the Dutch De Stijl, an early modernist movement.

Hawaii, with its lush soil and greenery, offered the antithesis of the machine. Willis began designing: a bar and tables for the "Shell Bar" of the Sheraton Hawaiian Village Hotel, being developed by Henry Kaiser. Featuring sandcasting imbedded

with Pacific Ocean seashells, the project used a variety of indigenous materials and organic forms. (It later became the stage set for the television series "Hawaii 5-0.")

Willis worked closely with Kaiser, who became a role model. He possessed the mettle and aggression of the oil-field hands but also owned a contracting company, a cement mill, and aluminum, steel, and automotive factories. Kaiser was equally drawn to Willis, who shared his entrepreneurial spirit. Their conversations gave Willis an insight into a scale of operation that helped her fuse her interests in art and building.

Willis returned to San Francisco in 1960—still with no formal architectural education—with a new sense of mission. She continued to pursue her many interests and talents, now compressed and distilled by her Hawaiian experience. Willis opened a self-styled design firm that took on an array of projects: furniture design, a set of mixed-media panels for United Air Lines, the renovation of a supermarket display, and the design of office interiors. She embraced the design tenets of the early sixties: good design equaled profit, and Willis soon profited from her talents.

Meanwhile, the population of San Fran-

cisco had swollen during the postwar years, and the city was entering the early phases of a preservation and renovation boom—a movement that foreshadowed similar efforts across the country. Willis, despite her rural sensibility, began to immerse herself in urban designs. She found that her interests ran parallel to those of local architects like William Wurster, who designed Ghiradelli Square, and Joseph Esherick, who designed the Cannery.

Six young entrepreneurs commissioned Willis to convert three small Victorian buildings into a complex that included several stores and two restaurants. The result influenced the design of Union Street between Gough and Pierce streets as it is today. Willis preserved the original buildings but jacked them up an entire story so that she could add an extra floor below. Willis's masterful and unabashed blend of marketing and architecture was an aesthetic and commercial success. As such adaptive reuse of historic structures proved profitable, the movement gradually flowed east, influencing the adaptation of Faneuil Hall and other sites.

Meanwhile, Willis's ebullience and energy continued to push her into new arenas. Still unwilling to confine herself to a single

reality. — PIET MONDRIAN • *As a rather special kind of mythic medium, science should communicate meaning to the widest pos*

focus, Willis opened a gourmet cookware store on Union Street. The shop, which Willis finally sold in 1970, was a financial watershed.

By 1966, Willis, in her mid-thirties, was a licensed architect and the only woman in San Francico with her own firm. Her work increasingly took precedence over her personal life. In building, she could create an ideal environment—one devoid of the conventional domestic role—a tradition that she felt had failed in her own childhood home.

As a woman without the traditional architectural academic training, Willis felt uncomfortable within the strict borders of architectural practice in San Francisco. Instead, she cultivated a social life similar to that of her early life in Hawaii. She spent time with developers, businessmen, and political figures, as well as with architects, and she inevitably entered the politics of architecture and planning. Willis served on the United States delegation to the United Nations conference on "Habitat" and became a trustee and founder of the National Building Museum in 1976 and the president of the California Chapter of the American Institute of Architects in 1979. Her work became more politically engaged as she took on projects nationwide.

As the firm grew to thirty-five people, Willis began working on several large-scale prototype buildings, including an unbuilt design for nine regional computer centers for the Internal Revenue Service. Her belief that a universal set of principles could guide architecture was expressed most clearly in her early work with computers. Here she could also address the issues that most affect building a new world on an enormous scale: planning, density, and land-use economics.

CARLA (Computerized Approach to Residential Land Analysis)—a computer program that Willis developed with Eric Tiescholz and Jochen Eigen—comes from a time when many felt that architecture could engineer the social fabric with machinelike efficiency. Willis's firm was one of the first to explore such systems across regional boundaries. CARLA received national attention and was used all over the country, including back in Hawaii.

Willis returned to Hawaii to work on a project unimaginable twenty years earlier, when she first came to the islands. She now worked on the scale of the social engineer, designing 525 buildings, nestled in the crater of an inactive volcano, for some 12,000 residents. CARLA pro-

grammed the density and siting to ensure that the results were "ecologically scientific," taking into account simple landscape issues that had been all but forgotten by developers who were essentially strip-mining plots of land throughout the sixties and seventies. The project was constructed in less than two years.

Such large-scale projects culminated in the design of the San Francisco Ballet Association Building. Completed in 1984, this was the second building added to the city's historic, French neo-Renaissance Civic Center. Fusing many of her ideas, the ballet building was a prototypical machine for dance that also responded—if abstractly—to the local scale and proportions.

Despite the growth of her firm, Willis adjusted her interests once again. The economy of the eighties entered a tailspin, and large projects (most notably the 24-acre Yerba Buena Gardens redevelopment project in the heart of San Francisco) were stalled or canceled. Moreover, San Francisco was far from the intellectual debates that were beginning to stir up the profession. Willis, secure in her professional and financial accomplishments, increasingly wanted to engage these discussions directly.

Her trips to the northeast seacoast

nce. — ROBERT HAMILTON • *It is never safe to look into the future with eyes of fear.* — EDWARD H. HARRIMAN • *Every chalice is a*

became more frequent and lasted longer. In 1991, she moved to New York City permanently. Two years later, Willis was awarded the Montgomery Fellowship at Dartmouth College. Her work there, primarily her featured lecture, led her to a reappraise the images that inspired her career and work and generated the underlying theme of this book.

Willis's eclectic experiences encouraged her to grapple with many facets of art and architecture as well as to confront the practicalities of building. Yet the consistency of her underlying images make the work coherent. These images are the memories that drove Willis to design.

Nicolai Ouroussoff

[Editor note: Beverly Willis, FAIA, is a founder and Director of the Architectural Research Institute, Inc., New York City. The Institute is a think/act tank that examines the rapid and diverse changes associated with the Information Age and their effects on architecture and urbanism. The Institute is a 501(c)(3) nonprofit educational organization.]

dwelling-place. — JEAN LAROCHE • *I don't want to be a genius—I have enough problems just trying to be a man.* — ALBERT CAM

Beverly Willis at left with Dartmouth College students. Courtesy of Stuart Bratesman, Dartmouth College.

Several years ago, when I embarked on the path that led to this book, I had no idea of the twists and turns that lay ahead. Reconciling in concept and illustration the diverse elements of the book's art, architecture, and writing did not come easily or quickly. Throughout, my friends and colleagues were indefatigably available and supportive.

The original text ideas and graphic presentation were kindled while preparing my Montgomery Fellowship lecture at Dartmouth College in the winter of 1992, titled "Mixed Messages: The Nonverbal Language of Art and Architecture."

Professor Ben Moss, then chairman of Dartmouth's Studio Art Department, sponsored my appointment and became a sounding board for these ideas. I am deeply grateful for his generosity of mind, spirit, and time.

I am indebted to writer-architect Sandra Hemingway for her contributions to the text, the book layout, and her ideas for illustrations. Her keen insight identified the key connections between the multiple aspects of my work and how best to present it. The page design was her idea, though author/designer Anistatia R. Miller is responsible for the overall design of the book. Sandra Hemingway organized the pages using two overlapping golden section diagrams that permit an inexhaustible number of arrangements. Architect Rick Rosson, editor Lois Nesbitt, and author/editor Jared M. Brown contributed additional graphic and editorial ideas. I owe a special thanks to David Morton, who recommended Anistatia R Miller to me and generously shared his publishing knowledge.

While the text of the book, design theory, artwork, and architectural design are my own work, their representation (the graphics, line drawings, and photographs that illustrate the work) is mostly the work of others. I have listed their names under "Contributors to Projects." To all I express my deepest gratitude.

This book is rooted in thoughts I had tried to articulate prior to the Montgomery Fellowship lecture. Certain people have been involved since these earliest conceptions. I am deeply indebted to Professor John McDermott, former Dean of the School of Architecture at University of Texas at Arlington, for his long-term support and advice, as well as to Professor Steven Hurtt, Dean of Architecture, University of Maryland; Professor Steven Sachs and historian Thomas Schumacher, University of Maryland; historian Diane Favro, University of California at Los Angeles; Professor Lars Lerup, Dean of Architecture, Rice University; architect-professor Stanley Saitowitz, University of California at Berkeley; Paolo Polledri, former curator of design and architecture, San Francisco Museum of Modern Art; and Lian Hurst Mann, contributing editor at *Architectural Record Magazine*, all of whom read and commented on the early drafts.

I am particularly indebted to Dr. Forrest Wilson, writer, lecturer, and educator, who guided me through many difficult stages of development and who contributed the wisdom and experience he has gained through writing and publishing many books on art and architecture. To create this book, I had to face some painful aspects of long buried childhood memories. For this, I am indebted to Dr. Wilson, Nicolai Ouroussoff (who wrote a biographical essay), and Kathleen Kelley.

During the development of the book, I moved my primary residence from San Francisco to New York, where I had the

...men who make history have not time to write it. — METTERNICH • *Order is not repetition. It is a central idea.* — LOUIS KAHN • *A*

opportunity to interact with a group of architects and designers who inspired me to broaden my view and see my work as a whole. I especially thank artist-designer-professor Sheila Levrant de Bretteville, Yale University; landscape architect Diana Balmori; professor-architect Lynne Breslin, Columbia University; Susana Torre, former Dean of Architecture, Parsons School of Design; Professor Jennifer Bloomer, Iowa State University; and curator Mildred Friedman, formerly of the Walker Art Gallery in Minneapolis.

Editor-writer Cynthia Davidson and architect Peter Eisenman deserve a special thanks for their friendship and advice.

An architecture student, Mark Waldo, who became a professional during the development of this book, and my assistant, Kerri Lynn Jennings, were particularly helpful in assembling certain material, as were others. I thank you all.

I'd like to express my gratitude to my publisher, the National Building Museum, and its staff. Particularly, I'd like to thank Susan Henshaw Jones, Robert McLean, Kent Colton, Gil DeLorme, and editors Winifer Skattebol and Lois Nesbitt.

Over the great many years that this book has evolved, others not mentioned here were helpful. Please know that omissions are not intentional and due only to fading memory.

rock pile ceases to be a rock pile the moment a single man comtemplates it, bearing within him the image of a cathedral

The professionals listed worked on the projects illustrated in this book, 1955–1995.

PRINCIPAL ARCHITECTS
Beverly Willis
David Coldoff

ASSOCIATE ARCHITECTS
Charles Rueger, Jr.
Gary Johnson
Anne Ryan
Jochen Eigen
Robert A. Wolf

SENIOR ARCHITECTS
Rosemary Muller
Dennis Schmidt
Christopher Raker
Jack Young
Dan Holland
Michio Yamaguchi
Pamela Clayton

PROFESSIONAL STAFF
Robert Aiken
Tut Bartzen
Joanna Bianchi
Laura Blake
Candice Boyer
C.P. Hollins Braestrup
Barbara Burrin
Hercules Christofides
Karen De Casas
Richard Coxon
Derek Dutton
Valdemir Frank
David Garber
Aurora Garcia
Dennis Heath
Carol Henderson
Lucille Irwin
Philip Jacka
Joanne Jackson
Charles F. Kahn
Robert Lameris
Paul Loh
David Maughan
Saghi Moaren
Phillip Rossetti
Richard Rueffer
Jill Ryan
Carl Scholz
Arthur Seymour
Kathlene Sullivan
Jane K. Thompson
Jackie Veltman
Mark Waldo
William Walsh
La Verne Wells-Bowie
Patrice Wick
Kristin Woehl
Eric Freed

ARCHITECTURAL GRAPHICS AND MODELS
Tom Hoepf
Dan Luis
Sima Farrokhi
Victoria Reynolds
S. Jane Matthews
David Chun

ADMINISTRATION
Janette Ryan
Vivenne Stock
Maya Adiel
Patricia L. Hughes
Paula Cohen
Stephanie Sichel
Eve Bagell
Joseph McCann

NE DE SAINT-EXUPERY • *Man can only become what he is able to consciously imagine or to "image forth."* — DANE RUDHYAR

SAN FRANCISCO BALLET BUILDING

Located in San Francisco's Civic Center, the site for San Francisco Ballet Association building was very modest, compared to the adjacent block-sized site occupied by the Opera House, Symphony Hall, the Veterans' Memorial Building, and City Hall. The city developed a design criterion for the building. One objective was to achieve compatibility with the center's neoclassical design vocabulary. Consequently, a tripartite horizontal ordering system, derived from Renaissance principles, dominates the facade. Breaking with classical symmetry, the entry is on the corner, offering a unique, visible identity for the growing ballet company from the Van Ness Boulevard facades of the Opera and Symphony.

Completed in 1984, the 65,500-square-foot, free-standing, four-story building, which is 96 feet tall, accommodates a world-class ballet company and a school of 500 students. It includes an in-house medical facility, along with rehearsal, instructional, administrative, and supporting spaces.

Dancers spend at least six hours daily in their "house," although they perform on the Opera House stage. Anticipating the dancers' demanding physical activity, the architects studied the wide range of dancers' needs, such as the acoustical and lighting requirements of seven dance studios, positioning mirrors to provide unbroken images of lifts and jumps, and designing fluorescent lighting free of the stroboscopic flickering that causes dizziness during rehearsal. Natural light and operable windows are used throughout the interior to provide fresh outdoor air. This building was the first of its kind constructed in the U.S. for the exclusive use of an American ballet company.

MR. AND MRS. RICHARD GOEGLIEN POOL HOUSE AND SCULPTURE

On a site in the Napa Valley hills, near Yountville, Richard Goeglien envisioned a pool house whose design would commemorate the valley's original inhabitants while accommodating casual poolside entertaining and the functional necessities of showering and dressing.

On the structure's central north-south axis, a sculpture was designed to mark the place imagined to have been a Wappa Indian camping ground. A commemorative marker is placed over a spot thought to be a burial mound. The sculpture and the bas-relief details of the stuccoed pool house facade derive from universal mythology. The changing summer solstice shadows cast by a circular totem symbolize a spiritual passage to the heavens. Nomadic gatherers and hunters, the Wappa Indian tribe left little evidence of their cultural traditions and imagery.

A golden-section geometry generated all parts of the building, modulating the two squares of the floor plan with a trace of the roof to derive three distinct spaces: the main space for entertaining, and the other two smaller spaces for cooking, dressing, and bathing. In the vaulted center section, sliding doors are pocketed into the walls, dissolving the boundaries between pool and house. The 800-square-foot wood-frame and stucco structure was completed in 1988.

GREENWICH APARTMENT

Faced with an existing cramped, convoluted, two-story apartment layout in a condominium complex, the design optically improves and enhances the existing space with a minimum of reconstruction. The Greenwich apartment interior design captures the grand spaces and elegant living of nineteenth-century townhouses. Using scale and illusion and supplementing natural light with carefully placed artificial lighting, the modest 1,200-square-foot space appears far larger and more luxurious than the floor area and budget suggest.

Since the top-floor kitchen was part of the entry, all appliances were placed at or below counter level, creating an atmosphere of open hospitality rather than of functional utility. Oversized wall openings, *faux* materials and perspectives, trompe-l'oeil paintings, reflective surfaces, and architectural pilasters convey an illusion of spatial depth and material substance in what had been a typical thin-walled, low-ceilinged tract apartment development. The *faux* surfaces and trompe-l'oeil paintings were executed by artist Randolph Johnson.

UNION STREET STORES

Originally the owners of three deteriorating Victorian houses on Union Street in San Francisco planned to demolish the structures and build a new commercial retail building. Off-street parking requirements made new construction less attractive. However, redevelopment of the existing buildings would require additional square footage to achieve economic objectives.

Like New York or London townhouses that offer access to levels above and slightly below the street, the design elevated the buildings sufficiently to add a new floor of usable space at the foundation level while rebuilding the crumbling foundation.

The porches of the twin Queen Anne wedding cottages were connected and a new stair added that effectively weaves the three buildings into a single retail complex that initially consisted of two restaurants, and seven stores. Historic details, such as a found wrought-iron fencing and gaslights, were added to enhance the restored facades. The successful design captured the imagination of others who applied many of the adaptive reuse design concepts to other properties fronting on Union Street. Together these renovations made Union Street a premier neighborhood shopping area. The development of Ghiradelli Square, the Cannery, Jackson Square, and Union Street foretold the reawakening and widespread national interest in preservation beginning in the sixties. Investor-owners William and Dickie Quayle, Harry and Mildred Golsom, and William and Maggie Lacey commissioned the design.

NOB HILL COURT

Sited at the foot of Nob Hill in San Francisco, this forty-five-unit apartment building offers a quiet retreat, sheltered from the noise, pollution, and potential intrusion of urban life. A protected interior courtyard serves as a private residential garden, providing a secluded outdoor space for the residents. A two-story entrance lobby with its sweeping circular stair is connected to the ground level parking garage that forms the base of the building and the enclosed court.

Consisting of mostly of one-bedroom apartments, the plan was designed to function primarily as a large living room. Large windows flood the high ceiling interior with light; door and ceiling moldings provide rich details that contrast with the smooth plaster walls. Fireplaces contribute to the ambiance of gracious living, warmth, and serenity. The large walk-in closet and compartmentalized bathrooms provide privacy from the single living area with its pull-down wall beds. The mullioned patterns of the wood window frames are similar to those found in single-family homes. Originally designed for investor Dorothy Fritz, the apartments were later converted to condominiums.

SHOWN WINERY

The unbuilt Richard Shown Winery was to be located in Yountville, California. The vertical-grain redwood facade of its main building is fitted together like the staves of an oak cask, held rigidly in place by two large steel bands encircling the building under a tern metal roof. The building houses the stainless steel winemaking tanks. The crushing of the grapes is done outside and piped into the tanks inside. Wine-tasting events also occur outdoors, under the trellised circular patio at the front entry.

The design of the wine-making and storage areas incorporates energy conservation techniques that regulate the temperature within the main production building. Cool night air is drawn in at the base with a timed intake fan; the hot air of the day radiates out through the open vents in the cupola.

To maintain the constant temperature required in the aging process, the storage areas are designed as "caves." Computer analysis calculated the appropriate thermal mass and number of air changes necessary to maintain a constant 50-to-60-degree temperature using passive cooling. Supported by a timed night air intake fan rather than air-conditioning, the system meets the strict temperature criteria while reducing energy consumption.

RIVER RUN RESIDENCE

Two small knolls, overlooking the Napa Valley on one side and the Napa River on the other, form the focus of the River Run ranch in St. Helena. Surrounded by a working vineyard of Cabernet Sauvignon grapes, the first knoll is occupied by the estate's remodeled gatehouse; the second, by a new 4,000-square-foot manor house and a separate guest house with a wine cellar and spa. Between the knolls are two barns. One was remodeled as a stable with a full tack room and grooming area; the other houses farm machinery.

The house's floor plan is comprised of four "living centers": the public reception and entertainment area, the food preparation and casual relaxation area, the semi-private library and study area, and the private sleeping and bath areas. The master bedroom fireplace is shared with the master bath. Both have a view of the vineyard. A pool and patio link the guest and main houses.

The house is approached in front by a looping drive ending in an oval turnaround. Semicircular stairs, beginning at each end, lead to a single flight of stairs ending at a columnated porch with its symmetrically placed front entry door. From the circular stairs, a wall of water cascades over a section of the patio-pool retaining wall, flowing into a semicircular fountain whose water is recycled to the pool above. However, the pool itself does not come into view until the patio level is reached. The pool itself consists of three parts: an eight-foot-square area; a long eight-foot wide by four-foot deep lap pool; and a shallow reflecting pool that provides the falling water that feeds the fountain below.

PACIFIC POINT CONDOMINIUMS

Ninety-eight condominium apartments for moderate-income buyers offer a spectacular 270-degree view of the Pacific Ocean. Geological conditions required minimizing potential damage from earthquakes, mud slides, and soil erosion, further determining the siting of individual buildings. CARLA—a proprietary computer program for residential land analysis—was used to devise a site plan that maximized views while positioning the apartments on the bluff's slope.

The stepped slope was graded to accommodate eight basic building blocks with garages for each unit, a recreational center, tennis courts, outdoor play spaces, and visitor parking. To meet construction cost criteria, the rectangular building blocks repeat basic floor plans and component parts, simplifying construction. To diminish the appearance of repetitiveness and provide privacy between the apartments, building walls protrude through the front and rear facades. When the building is rotated several degrees from the parallel position, each wall like the ribs of a fan unfolding in different directions points to a particular view.

Located in Pacifica, California, the buildings contain two floor plans, one with two bedrooms and two baths, the other with two bedrooms and one bath. All of the condominiums have double stud walls, as well as lightweight concrete floors and acoustical insulation at all common floors and walls, virtually eliminating sound transference between apartments.

IRS COMPUTER CENTER BUILDING

Designed in 1976 for the General Services Administration for use by the Internal Revenue Service, the project was proposed as a prototypical computing center for construction in all nine regional IRS complexes scattered throughout the United States. A totally flexible building, the hexagonal shape adapts easily to multiple sites within the one story, flat roof building configurations of the nine different campuses.

Capable of accommodating one to four levels and different facade materials, the design incorporates energy conservation techniques, user-friendly task lighting and workstations, and flexible computer infrastructure developed for the project. The central open space—which can be built as either an open air courtyard or a domed atrium—increases the amount of light and air available to the occupants and provides a natural complement to the technology-driven building. The first prototype was proposed for the IRS campus at Covington, Kentucky, but remains unbuilt. The project was a joint venture with Coleman/Graves Architects.

CHILDREN'S RECREATIONAL CENTER

Located in a modest-income neighborhood in San Francisco, the Children's Recreational Center in the Margaret Hayward Park was designed as a toy building. Lower in height than the tallest of the playground equipment, the building unfolds from a corner of the site in a series of small spaces created by diagonally slanting wall planes. Facing the playground and wide steps, the front diagonal wall has an arched, for-children-only opening that encourages playful exploration and serves as a backdrop for impromptu performances or simply hanging out.

The layered wall planes also allow graduations in scale that accommodate both children and adults. Wide steps, linking the playground and building entrance, create an informal stage and child-size seating area. The 1,200-square-foot interior accommodates the main recreational playroom, administrative offices, and various support services.

MANHATTAN VILLAGE ACADEMY HIGH SCHOOL

Manhattan Village Academy, a 350-student high school, is located in midtown Manhattan's Chelsea's district in a tall, art-nouveau era building, originally a factory. Called an alternative high school, it is sponsored by both the Center for Collaborative Education and the Coalition of Essential Schools: an educational reform movement which is led by Ted Sizer and, in New York City, by Deborah Meier. Owned and administered by the City of New York Board of Education, its student body—like other New York public schools—is multicultural. In New York, the factory model plan with classrooms connected to lengthy, winding corridors did not fit the reform pedagogy.

The school's unique teaching process of personalized education—one which concentrates on projects designed to fit the abilities of students at all levels—required a different floor plan. The design needed to accommodate flexible spatial configurations that fit the teaching needs for a variety of individual and group projects. It also had to serve standard lecture requirements. From the requirements developed by Deborah Meier, and the school's principal Mary Butz, I created the Locus Plan. Each "locus" is the community center of an instructional cluster, an integrating court that houses student lockers and serves as both a meeting place and spatial core for the cluster. Adjacent to this, four interconnected classroom clusters—one allocated for a math/science room—are located around a multi-use interior quad. Each of these spaces forms a teaching center for a single grade level.